Multi-Ethnic Literature

☐ AFRO-AMERICAN AUTHORS

■ AMERICAN INDIAN AUTHORS

☐ ASIAN-AMERICAN AUTHORS

☐ MEXICAN-AMERICAN AUTHORS

☐ CHICANO VOICES

American

HOUGHTON
MIFFLIN
COMPANY

BOSTON
ATLANTA
DALLAS
GENEVA, ILL.
HOPEWELL, N. J.
PALO ALTO
TORONTO

Indian Authors

Natachee Scott Momaday

10892

ACKNOWLEDGMENTS

Grateful acknowledgment is made to authors, publishers, and agents for their permission to reprint the following selections.

"Achieving Manhood" and "Bear White Child," from *Two Leggings: The Making of a Crow Warrior,* by Peter Nabokov. Copyright © 1967 by Peter Nabokov. Reprinted by permission of Thomas Y. Crowell Company, Inc.

"The Bear and the Colt," from pp. 198–204 (under the title "The Bear and the Colt") from *House Made of Dawn,* by N. Scott Momaday. Copyright © 1967, 1968 by N. Scott Momaday. Reprinted by courtesy of Harper & Row, Publishers, Inc.

"Blood on the Little Bighorn," from *Winter Count,* by D. Chief Eagle. Copyright 1967 by D. Chief Eagle. Reprinted by permission of the Johnson Publishing Co. of Boulder, Colorado.

"Blue Winds Dancing," by Tom Whitecloud. First appeared in *Scribner's Magazine* (February 1939). Reprinted by permission of the author.

"The Butchering at Wounded Knee" and "The Killing of Crazy Horse," by John G. Neihardt. Reprinted from *Black Elk Speaks: Being the Life Story of a Holy Man of the Oglala Sioux,* as told through John G. Neihardt, by permission of the John G. Neihardt Trust. Copyright 1932, 1959 by John G. Neihardt. Copyright © 1961 by the University of Nebraska Press. No part of this book in excess of 250 words may be reproduced in any form without permission in writing from the publisher.

"The Changer Comes to the Lummi" and "The Maiden Sacrificed to Winter," from *Indian Legends of the Pacific Northwest,* by Ella E. Clark. Originally published by the University of California Press. Copyright 1953 by The Regents of the University of California, and reprinted by their permission.

"Chee's Daughter," by Juanita Platero and Siyowin Miller, from *Common Ground,* Vol. VIII (Winter 1948). Reprinted by permission of the American Council for Nationalities Service.

"Death in the Woods," by Littlebird, from *The American Indian Speaks,* edited by John R. Milton. Published by Dakota Press. Copyright © 1969 by the University of South Dakota. Reprinted by permission of the publisher.

"Direction," by Alonzo Lopez, from *The American Indian Speaks,* edited by John R. Milton. Published by Dakota Press. Copyright © 1969 by the University of South Dakota. Reprinted by permission of the publisher.

From *The Way to Rainy Mountain,* by N. Scott Momaday. Copyright © 1969 by the University of New Mexico Press. Reprinted by permission of the publisher.

"The Hunter and His Dogs" and "The Orphan," from *Myths and Tales of the Southeastern Indians* (Smithsonian Institution, Bureau of American Ethnology, Bulletin 88), by John R. Swanton. Reprinted by permission of the Smithsonian Institution Press.

"I Do Have a Name," from *Miracle Hill: The Story of a Navaho Boy,* by Emerson Blackhorse Mitchell and T. D. Allen. Copyright 1967 by the University of Oklahoma Press. Reprinted by permission of the publisher.

"The Man from Washington," by James Welch. Reprinted by permission of the author.

"Navaho Chant," from *The Dîné: Origin Myths of the Navaho Indians* (Smithsonian Institution, Bureau of American Ethnology, Bulletin 163), by Aileen O'Bryan. Reprinted by permission of the Smithsonian Institution Press.

Library of Congress Catalog Card Number: 78-160036

ISBN: 0–395–24040–9

PHOTO CREDITS

Contents

INTRODUCTION   1

Chief Joseph   5
  "Of One Mind"   5

Legends   7
  The Changer Comes to the Lummi   7
  The Maiden Sacrificed to Winter   10
  The Orphan   13
  The Hunter and His Dogs   16

Papago War Song   18

Two Leggings   20
  Bear White Child   21
  Achieving Manhood   27

D. Chief Eagle   29
  Blood on the Little Bighorn   30

Black Elk   38
  The Killing of Crazy Horse   39
  The Butchering at Wounded Knee   43

Charles A. Eastman   49
  On the White Man's Trail   50

Thomas S. Whitecloud   60
  Blue Winds Dancing   61

Alonzo Lopez   69
  Direction   69

Emerson Blackhorse Mitchell and T. D. Allen   70
    I Do Have a Name   71

Patty Harjo   79
    Who Am I?   79

Juanita Platero and Siyowin Miller   81
    Chee's Daughter   81

Navaho Chant   95

Durango Mendoza   96
    Summer Water and Shirley   96

Grey Cohoe   106
    The Promised Visit   106

Littlebird   117
    Death in the Woods   117

N. Scott Momaday   119
    The Bear and the Colt   119
    From *The Way to Rainy Mountain*   125

James Welch   132
    The Man from Washington   132

Vine Deloria, Jr.   133
    This Country Was a Lot Better Off When
    the Indians Were Running It   133

The Whole World Is Coming   145

    MAJOR TRIBES IN THE UNITED STATES   148

About the Author

NATACHEE SCOTT MOMADAY

 Born in Fairview, Kentucky, of Cherokee, French, and English descent, Natachee Scott Momaday has attained distinction as an artist, a teacher, and an author of books for young people. She received her education at Haskell Junior College, Crescent College, the University of New Mexico, and the University of California at Los Angeles. As an artist, she has exhibited works in oil, charcoal, pastels, and pen and ink. Formerly a teacher in reservation schools and a long-time resident of Jemez Pueblo, Mrs. Momaday now prepares curriculum materials for the schools of Gallup, New Mexico. She has written numerous articles and short stories dealing with the culture of the American Indian. Her works for young people include the novel *Owl in the Cedar Tree* as well as stories written especially for students in the Kayenta, Arizona, schools. In 1968 the New Mexico Press Women gave Mrs. Momaday an award as the outstanding woman writer in the state, and in 1975 the University of New Mexico honored her with a doctorate in humane letters.

Introduction

American Indian literature grew out of an oral tradition passed on from generation to generation. By the late eighteenth century these oral accounts of Indians' life stories and views were being recorded or translated by interested white people. At this time Indians were also beginning to write down their own histories in the white man's language. And by the twentieth century creativity in the English language became a prevalent form of their literary communication.

The Indian has always used words with reverence and awe, weaving them into chants and songs to create beauty and to express his daily needs and aspirations. He may weave words into patterns of power against his enemy, as in the Papago War Song on page 18. N. Scott Momaday captures the essence of the Indian attitude toward words when he describes an old woman in his novel *House Made of Dawn:* "For her words were medicine; they were magic and invisible. They came from nothing into sound and meaning. They were beyond price; they could neither be bought nor sold. And she never threw them away." The Indians' attitude toward words is, in a sense, an extension of their philosophy of the world about them—that one should revere rather than waste or destroy the natural beauty of the universe.

Oral literature assumed the forms of legends, ceremonial chants and prayers, and poems. Legends, still greatly respected by many Indians, frequently revolve around encounters with supernatural beings and are often explanations of how natural elements such as fire came about, as in the legend "The Changer Comes to the Lummi" (page 7). Animals are sometimes represented humorously as people, as Rabbit appears in "The Orphan" (page 13). Indian chants and poems were often created in praise of or asking for special powers from deified elements of nature.

1

With the coming of the white man, historical and biographical recordings became an integral part of American Indian literature. Indians often told their life stories to anthropologists or settlers through interpreters; the book *Two Leggings: The Making of a Crow Warrior*, for example, tells as much about the culture of the Crow tribe as it does of the warrior Two Leggings. Religious philosophy of the Sioux tribe is interspersed with accounts of historical conflicts with white men during the last half of the nineteenth century in such books as D. Chief Eagle's *Winter Count* and John G. Neihardt's *Black Elk Speaks*. The white man was technologically superior to the Indians and won these conflicts; and the Indians' despair in losing their freedom and their land is reflected in many of these narratives. As the medicine man Black Elk said when he recounted the massacre of several hundred Sioux at Wounded Knee, South Dakota, ". . . the nation's hoop is broken and scattered."

By 1890 most Indians had been placed on reservations and were "adjusting" to a new form of existence. Some, like author Charles Eastman, were "on the white man's trail," learning the values of the white man's civilization. Others, like Thomas Whitecloud, found it difficult to assimilate the white man's ways and still followed their own tribal cultures. Dr. Whitecloud's autobiographical essay "Blue Winds Dancing" (page 61) provides an effective contrast to Eastman's acceptance of white society. A college student when he wrote the essay, Dr. Whitecloud found campus life "artificial" and longed for the peace and happiness he felt when with his people on his home reservation, where existence was closely related to the natural environment.

The last half of the twentieth century is witnessing the Indians' adoption of the English language as a creative form of communication: American Indian fiction, nonfiction, and poetry abound. Interestingly enough, most authors have maintained the basic cultures of their tribes, but the traditional is now employed in an original and creative sense. Elements that occurred in legends, such as the supernatural, appear as themes in such stories as Durango Mendoza's "Summer Water and Shirley" (page 96), in which a spell is cast upon a little girl, and in Grey Cohoe's "The Promised Visit" (page 106), where a young man driving home in a thunderstorm encounters a beautiful and mysterious young woman.

The traditional reverence for nature is a characteristic of many Indian authors' works. In Juanita Platero and Siyowin Miller's "Chee's Daughter" (page 81), Chee's belief in the land as a regenerative force is tested. N. Scott Momaday in "The Bear and the Colt" (page 119) writes of the natural bond of the hunter and the hunted. Much contemporary poetry also deals with the eternal theme of man's relationship with nature.

Perhaps the greatest innovation in American Indian thought has occurred within the past few years, with the advent of Red Power —a political and social movement indicative of a rebirth of pride in Indians themselves as well as greater respect accorded to them by other members of society. This movement has inevitably affected American Indian literature. Such writers as James Welch, expressing the bitterness felt by many Indians as a result of their treatment in the past, are rapidly gaining prominence on the American literary scene. Vine Deloria, Jr., an outstanding social commentator with a provocative sense of humor, is perhaps the best-known literary proponent of the Red Power movement, as evidenced in his books *Custer Died for Your Sins: An Indian Manifesto; We Talk, You Listen: New Tribes, New Turf;* and *God Is Red.* Deloria comments on the Indians' nature: "It is this special pride and dignity, the determination to judge life according to one's own values and the unconquerable conviction that the tribes will not die, that has always characterized Indian people. . . ."

Surely, throughout American Indian literature, from legends to contemporary creative works, one unifying factor is the "special pride and dignity" Deloria mentions. In the early literature this dignity was evidenced as a cultural phenomenon, where self-identity was bound to tribal membership. During the twentieth century the works of American Indian authors have assumed a more individualistic tone: while the tribe is often recognized as a major cultural influence, authors no longer consider themselves solely as spokesmen for a larger group. But in maintaining the distinctive features of their culture in their literature throughout its history, Indians' contribution to American literature as a whole has indeed been unique. Ironically it is only now that the American public is recognizing the important part played in the development of our national literary heritage by the American Indians, the first Americans.

LOCATIONS REFERRED TO IN THE TEXT

4

Chief Joseph

1840?–1904

From the time the Lewis and Clark Expedition entered Wallowa Valley (now part of Idaho) in 1805, the white man and the Nez Percé Indians had been friends. Chief Joseph and his tribe lived peacefully in this green land of mountain forests and winding rivers. Yet, in 1877, when gold was discovered in nearby mountains and more and more settlers were moving into this area, the Government began to pressure Chief Joseph to sign treaties which would restrict him and his people to a reservation. When Chief Joseph refused, fighting broke out between settlers and Indians, and war was declared. Although greatly outnumbered, the Nez Percé managed to harass and evade United States troops in a heroic 1300-mile retreat toward Canada. They were finally surrounded fifty miles from their destination, and the majority of them were ultimately settled in Lapwai Reservation in Idaho. Chief Joseph, however, never again saw the beloved land of Wallowa Valley.

"Of One Mind"

The earth was created by the assistance of the sun, and it should be left as it was. . . . The country was made without lines of demarcation, and it is no man's business to divide it. . . . I see the whites all over the country gaining wealth, and see their desire to give us lands which are worthless. . . . The earth and myself are of one mind. The measure of the land and the measure of our bodies are the same. Say to us, if you can say it, that you were sent by the Creative Power to talk to us. Perhaps you think the Creator sent you here to dispose of us as you see fit. If I thought you were sent by the Creator, I might be induced to think you had a right to dispose of me. Do not misunderstand me, but understand me fully with reference to my affection for the land. I never said the land was mine to do with it as I chose. The one who has the right to dispose of it is the one who has created it. I claim a right to live on my land, and accord you the privilege to live on yours.

Legends

One of the earliest forms of Indian literature, legends are stories transmitted by word of mouth from generation to generation among tribes. It is an old Indian custom to teach through stories, and many legends are used to instruct and to reaffirm the culture of the group. Only in the last hundred years have legends been written down; most of them have been recorded by anthropologists studying Indian society.

The following selections are representative legends of four tribes —Lummi, Chinook, Alabama, and Hitchiti. "The Changer Comes to the Lummi" and "The Maiden Sacrificed to Winter" are from Indian Legends of the Pacific Northwest *by Ella E. Clark. "The Orphan" and "The Hunter and His Dogs" are from John R. Swanton's* Myths and Tales of the Southeastern Indians.

The Changer Comes to the Lummi

Lummi Tribe

Long, long ago, when the Changer was on the earth, the Lummi Indians of the northern Puget Sound shores heard of his coming. He was traveling among the islands, they were told, in a canoe that moved itself without paddles. Everywhere he went, he was kind to the people, healing the sick and helping the fishermen with their nets. He had the strength of four men, and he could control the winds and the waters.

7

When the Lummi heard that he was near, they began to get ready for a big feast in his honor. They caught ducks with their nets. They dug clams, gathered crabs, and caught fresh salmon. The women dug fern roots and gathered the summer berries.

At that time people did not know how to make fire. Some of the food was eaten raw. Some of it was cooked by the heat of the sun. Fresh salmon was placed in a cedar bowl filled with water, and the bowl was tipped so that the sun's rays would reach it. As they prepared the feast for the Changer, girls danced round the bowl chanting, "Cook quickly! Cook quickly! Cook quickly!" All day they danced and chanted, from early morning until sunset.

On the morning that the Changer was expected, all the people painted their faces with special care. The men put on their long buckskin shirts, which they wore only for ceremonies. The women put on their fringed cedar-bark skirts. The maidens braided their hair with flowers. Mats were placed on the shore for the Changer to walk on.

Again the cedar bowls of food were tilted toward the sun. Again the maidens began their dance and chant: *"Hwonk, quence, quell! Hwonk, quence, quell!"* ("Cook quickly! Cook quickly! Cook quickly!")

Suddenly the Changer landed on the shore. He saw the mats which had been spread for him. He heard the chanting and saw the dancing. He walked over to the open place where the girls were singing.

"What are they doing, my friends?"

The chief of the village answered him. "A special meal is being cooked for you by our daughters. We wish you to eat with us. We have been waiting for you."

The Changer's heart was touched. "I will gladly eat with you. And in return for your kindness I will give you a great gift. I will show you how to make fire. No longer will you need to dance and pray for the sun to cook your food."

The girls stopped their dancing and chanting. All the people watched while the Changer took a little stick with a hollow in it. This he placed upon the ground. He filled the hollow with some dry, crushed cedar bark. Then he took a sharp stick and twirled the end of it against the cedar bark, rubbing his hands together with the stick between them. Soon there was heat, and a thin curl of smoke began to rise. The cedar bark was on fire.

Then the Changer selected the strongest young man in the village, one skillful with bow and arrow. He put the sharpened stick between the palms of his hands and showed him how to make fire for his people.

The footprints of the Changer can still be seen on the shores of Chuckanut Bay.

FOR DISCUSSION

What do you think is the purpose of this legend?

The Maiden Sacrificed to Winter

Chinook Tribe

A winter colder and harder than any before came to the land of the Chinook people. Snow lay on the level as deep as half a man's height. The time for spring came, but the snow did not melt. Ice floated down the river in huge masses, grinding and crashing. Every night more snow fell, filling up places the wind had swept clean. Snowbirds were everywhere.

One day a bird flew over with something red in its bill. The people so frightened it that it dropped the red thing—a ripe strawberry. Then they knew that somewhere not far away spring had come. Around them it was still winter. The earth was frozen.

Something was wrong. So the chief of the village called a meeting at his lodge. All the people came. The old men asked each other, "Why does the winter not end? What can we do to end it?"

After much talk, the oldest man in the village arose and spoke. "Our grandfathers used to say that if a bird should be struck by a stone, the snow would never stop falling. Perhaps some child has stoned a bird."

The headman asked that all the children be brought in before the council. When they came, they were questioned one by one. Each child spoke for himself. Every mother was in fear, lest her child be the guilty person. One by one, the children said they had not struck any bird. Some of them pointed to a little girl. "She did it."

"You ask your daughter if the children speak the truth," the old men of the council said to her father and mother.

In terror the little girl answered that she had struck a bird with a stone.

The chief men of the village sat in council for a long time. The child and her parents waited, trembling.

Slowly the chief arose. "Give us your child. We will not kill her as we first thought we would do. Instead, we will give her to Winter. Then he will cease to be angry, and Summer will come."

The hearts of the little girl's father and mother were sad and heavy. This was their only child. But they realized that the wise men of the village knew best, and that the good of all was more important than the life of their little one. Many people brought them gifts in payment for the child, but their hearts were not lightened. As the headmen led her away, her father and mother cried aloud. They mourned for her as if for the dead.

Some young men were sent to the river to get a large block of ice. The headmen would place the maiden on it and thus give her to Winter. Finding a large piece in an eddy in the river, they pulled it to shore.

While the young men did that, all the other people dressed in their finest clothes, as if for the winter dances. The little girl was dressed best of all. Then the headmen led her to the river, and all the people followed.

At the water's edge they spread a thick layer of straw on the block of ice, and over that a covering of many tule[1] mats. They placed the girl on the ice and pushed it out into the swift current. Swirling with the rise and fall of the water, the ice block drifted down the river. The crying of the child and the wailing of the parents could be heard above the noise of the water and the crashing of the ice. When child and ice block were out of sight, the people returned to their lodges, chanting.

Very soon they felt a warm wind. In a few days the snow had gone. Then the people knew that the old men of years gone by had spoken the truth.

When spring came, the people moved to their fishing place to catch and dry the salmon. In the fall they went back to their winter village. Snow and ice came again. One day some old men stood by the riverbank watching the ice drift by. Far down the stream, as far as their eyes could see, a block of ice swirled round and round in an eddy. On the ice was a black spot.

The headmen of the village sent a young man out to look at it. "It looks like a body!" he called back as he drew near the ice block. The people who were watching brought long poles and drew the ice to the shore. On it was a young girl—the one who had been sacrificed as an offering to Winter.

---

[1] TULE (tōō´lē): bulrush; grasslike plant which grows in marshes.

The people lifted her up and carried her to the lodge of her father and mother. Wrapped in warm furs, she fell asleep by the fire.

Ever after that, she was able to walk barefoot on ice and snow. People thought she had special power. They called her *Wah-kah-nee,* meaning "She drifts."

FOR DISCUSSION

What does this Chinook legend tell us about the tribe's form of government? How are justice and mercy incorporated within the system?

The Orphan

Alabama Tribe

A youth without father or mother was dressed up by those who had the care of him. He was a poor boy, but he had on fine clothes. Then they sent him away. At some distance he got arrows and a bow, and after traveling on for some time, met a girl. She told him she wanted him to shoot a dove sitting on a tree close by. He did so and gave it to her. "That is all right," he thought. He started on again and met another woman. She asked the same favor, and he gratified her also.

Going on again he met Rabbit, who was wearing a deerhide, and they traveled in company. They came to a pond to hunt terrapin,[1] and when they got there, Rabbit tied up his white deerhide around the youth's fine clothes. Then both prepared to dive under water. The youth dived first and hunted about for terrapin. Rabbit also dived, but came out quickly and carried off the white deerhide and all of the clothing. Without much trouble the orphan got many terrapin, tied them up, and brought them out of the water. He came out carrying them tied up with a rope. Then he saw that Rabbit had run off with his shirt, leaving an old shirt for him. He put it on and set out.

By and by the youth came to where a persimmon[2] tree stood, shook it, and picked up and ate a great deal of the fruit. Some of the fruit he mashed up in his hands and rubbed all over his shirt. Having done so, he took the terrapin and started on.

On the way he stopped at a certain house and remained standing outside. A young girl came out. Then she went back and said to her mother, "Look out here." Her mother did so and said, "Go and speak to him." So she went and said to him, "Come in." There was a bed all ready for him to lie down on, but he did not want to lie down because his body was covered with persimmon juice. He moved the bed away and sat down on the other side on the

---

[1] TERRAPIN (tĕr'ə•pən): turtles.
[2] PERSIMMON: red-orange fruit resembling a plum.

floor. Then he said to the girl, "I have three or four terrapin out-side." She went to the place and brought them back to her mother, and they cooked and ate them. All were very much pleased, and he married that girl.

At the end of four or five days the youth and his wife prepared to go to the water, to the creek. The young man said, "Comb your hair." After she had done so, the two set out for the water. There he dived back and forth under water four or five times and came out, and they started back. Then he said to his wife, "Go and tell your relatives to go and look at the place in the creek where I dived." They did so and found quantities of fish all over the water. They brought baskets into which to put them. Then they cooked all the fish and ate them.

After this the young man said to his wife again, "Comb your hair." The two went to the water, and when they had gotten there and she had washed her hair, numbers of lice fell out which turned into fish. Then they went back to the house, and she said to the people, "Take your baskets and go to the water to see what is in it." They took their baskets, and when they got to the place, they picked up numbers of fish, filled their baskets, put them on their backs, carried them home, and cooked and ate them.

Rabbit heard what he had done and tried to imitate him. He took his wife to the creek, dived back and forth, and told his wife to tell her relations to go to the water and look. But when they arrived, they found nothing.

Afterwards the orphan went hunting and traveled along near the creek. He killed a deer and hung its body upon a tree. Presently he killed another, which he treated in the same manner, and he did this repeatedly. When he had gotten home, he said, "Let your people follow around where I have been hunting." They took a horse and set out, and coming to where the first deer was hung up, they laid the carcass upon the horse. They loaded the other deer upon his back in the same manner and returned home.

Then Rabbit also went hunting, and when he came to the place where the orphan had killed his first deer, he found the liver which had been thrown away, cut it into small pieces, and hung them up. At each place where a deer had been killed, he did the same thing, and when he got back, he said to his wife, "Let your people hunt where I have been." They did so, but found only small pieces of liver to bring home.

Next the orphan directed his wife to comb and part her hair and sit down near him, and when she had done so, he seized a stick and split her in two so cleverly that he now had two wives instead of one.

Rabbit heard of it and thought, "I will do the same thing. I will have my wife sit down with her hair combed and parted and will hit her with a stick in the same manner." But when he tried it, his wife fell down dead.

Then Rabbit ran away and was pursued by men with dogs. After he had been pursued for a long time, he took refuge in a hollow tree, and the men stationed Blue Crane in front of it to watch him while they went for an ax. The Crane was given a rope with which to tie Rabbit in case he tried to escape. But after the men were out of sight, Rabbit asked Crane to look inside. Then he asked him for the rope; and when Crane had given it to him, he tied it around his neck and fastened him to the tree, after which he procured a switch and beat him until he was black and blue and cried out, "Glo, glo, glo." Finally a person ran up in response to the cries, and Rabbit ran away.

After that Rabbit asked the orphan how he had made his house new, and he answered, "I renewed by cutting the house posts nearly through." So Rabbit chopped his house posts nearly through. He lay down inside, and about midnight the house fell down upon him.

FOR DISCUSSION

1. Is the orphan the hero because of his innate character, or simply because of his supernatural powers? Cite instances in the story which support your views.

2. What do you think is the intention of this Alabama Indian legend?

The Hunter and His Dogs

Hitchiti Tribe

A man having many dogs fell sick and lay in a helpless condition. One small puppy was able to talk with his master. Whatever the big dogs thought, they told to the puppy, and he in turn told his master all that had been said.

While they were there, the big dogs said to the puppy, "There is no food hereabouts. Tell him we can carry him along with us on a hunt if he agrees." The puppy told his master. He said, "They want me to tell you that we could take you hunting with us." When he told him that, the man answered, "You could not take me in any way." But the dogs said to the puppy again, "Tell him we know a way by which we can take him if he agrees to go." When he told his master, the latter said, "You may take me if you can think of a way." The puppy told the big dogs. "If that is so, we will take him with us," said the dogs.

They laid his gun on the bedding, and all seized the corners of the blanket under him, lifted it up, and went on with it. When they got far off, they stopped and made a camp and laid the man down; and the dogs collected wood for him. Then they built a fire, and while the man lay still, the dogs went out hunting for him. Each evening, when they came back, they brought some squirrels or turkeys they had killed, and he ate them. The man lying there got a little better.

While he was still in bed, the dogs said to the puppy, "Tell him we will move on again if he agrees." The puppy told his master. He said, "They say it is best to move." When the puppy told him, he said, "All right." So they seized the blanket again, carried him along, and made another camp. Laying the man down there, the dogs went hunting and returned in the evening with some squirrels or some turkeys they had killed or some tortoises they had found. The man ate them in bed and got better.

When he got up and could go about for short distances, the dogs went out hunting one morning, and he heard them barking not very far from camp. The puppy had remained with the man in camp. Then one dog came back on the run and said, "We have treed a bear, but we can't do anything with him. I have come to see if our master cannot come to that place, which is only a short distance away." He told this to the little dog, and the puppy told it to his master. "If I go slowly, I may be able to get there," said the man. The puppy said, "He says, 'I will go.'" When he told the other dog, he ran back again and informed the rest. "He is going to come," he said.

So the dogs waited and kept watch on the bear. When the man and the puppy got there, they brought the man's gun. The man shot down the bear which they had treed, skinned it, and cut it up. Then the dogs seized the pieces thus cut up and carried them all back to camp. They had plenty of meat.

"Now I am well," said the man. "Let us go home." He said to the puppy, "Tell the big dogs." The puppy said to the dogs, "He wants me to say to you, 'We must go home,'" and the big dogs said, "All right; but tell him when we get there and his former mother-in-law wants to give him something to eat, before he eats, he must let us eat." So he told his master. "This is what I have been told to say," he said to his master. "All right," he said, and they started on.

When they reached his home, his former mother-in-law set out something for him to eat. The man sat down to eat but remembered what the dogs had told him. The thought troubled him very much. He sat without eating. Then he saw the dogs looking at him. The puppy sat looking, and the man sitting there gave a piece of bread to each. The puppy took the bread, moved away, and sat down. As he sat crying, he fell over and died. All of the dogs sat down with their bread in the same way, cried, and died. It is said that all of them died.

This is how it is told.

FOR DISCUSSION

1. The hunter's dogs are his most faithful companions. How do they demonstrate their loyalty at the end of the story?

2. Compare this legend to "The Changer Comes to the Lummi," "The Maiden Sacrificed to Winter," and "The Orphan." Which legend seems to you to be the best told? Explain your answer.

Barely eking out an existence from the desert soil of southern Arizona, the Papagos never found cause to fight with the white man. Though a peaceful people, they occasionally did have battles with Apache neighbors and others who came to steal the products of a harvest. At these times war was a serious business, fought neither for personal nor tribal glory, but for instilling fear in the enemy so that future attacks would be discouraged. Many nights before each battle, a war orator would sing to the men of the tribe, calling them to their duty.

The following war song was collected by Ruth Murray Underhill and appeared in her book Singing for Power: The Song Magic of the Papago Indians of Southern Arizona.

Papago War Song

Is it for me to eat what food I have
And all day sit idle?
Is it for me to drink the sweet water poured out
And all day sit idle?
Is it for me to gaze upon my wife
And all day sit idle?
Is it for me to hold my child in my arms
And all day sit idle?

My desire was uncontrollable.
It was the dizziness (of battle);
I ground it to powder and therewith I painted my face.

It was the drunkenness (of battle);
I ground it to powder and therewith I tied my hair in a war
  knot.
Then did I hold firm my well-covering shield and my hard-
  striking club.

Then did I hold firm my well-strung bow and my smooth,
    straight-flying arrows.
To me did I draw my far-striding sandals, and fast I tied them.

Over the flat land did I then go striding,
Over the embedded stones did I then go stumbling,
Under the trees in the ditches did I go stooping,
Through the trees on the high ground did I go hurtling,
Through the mountain gullies did I go brushing quickly.

In four halts did I reach the shining white eagle, my guardian,
And I asked power.
Then favorable to me he felt
And did bring forth his shining white stone.
Our enemy's mountains he made white as with moonlight
And brought them close,
And across them I went striding.

In four halts did I reach the blue hawk, my guardian,
And I asked power.
Then favorable to me he felt
And did bring forth his blue stone.
Our enemy waters he made white as with moonlight,
And around them I went striding.

There did I seize and pull up and make into a bundle
Those things which were my enemy's,
All kinds of seeds and beautiful clouds and beautiful winds.
Then came forth a thick stalk and a thick tassel,
And the undying seed did ripen.

This I did on behalf of my people.
Thus should you also think and desire,
All you my kinsmen.

FOR DISCUSSION

Discuss the relationship of tribal duty and communal feeling to the last
stanza of the song. Would you consider this an effective war song?

Two Leggings

1844?–1923

Born along the banks of the Bighorn River in Montana, Two Leggings was a successful Crow warrior who learned to temper his innate courage with respect for the religious traditions of his tribe. As a boy he watched the older warriors carry out successful raids against other tribes, and it was his ambition to become not only a great warrior, but also a great chief. But only a warrior who experienced a great vision, sent from supernatural beings (the Without Fires) of the Other Side Camp, and confirmed through battle experience, was destined to become chief. Two Leggings fasted for long periods of time, steamed himself in sweat lodges,[1] and practiced many other forms of self-discipline and sacrifice which he hoped would bring forth the expected vision and confirm his power. However, the great vision never came to Two Leggings, and he never realized his ambition to become chief.

Two Leggings' life story ends in 1888, the year when he led a raid against the Sioux in what is believed to be the last Crow war party. Though he lived thirty-five years longer on a reservation, Two Leggings stated, "Nothing happened after that. We just lived. There were no more war parties, no capturing of horses from the Piegans[2] and the Sioux, no buffalo to hunt. There is nothing more to tell." When a Crow warrior is no longer permitted to fight, his life has essentially ended.

Two Leggings related his autobiography to William Wildschut, a Dutch-born businessman who also conducted various ethnological studies for The Museum of the American Indian, Heye Foundation. Wildschut's manuscript of these conversations remained unpublished in the Museum's archives until 1962, when Peter

[1] SWEAT LODGES: small oblong buildings in which steam was used to purify the body in religious rites.

[2] PIEGANS: members of one of the three tribes of the Blackfeet Confederacy.

Nabokov rediscovered it. A research assistant for the Museum, Mr. Nabokov had also worked for many years on Navaho,[3] Sioux, and Crow reservations. Recognizing the value of the document for anthropologist and layman alike, he re-edited the manuscript, providing it with greater accuracy and objectivity. Two Leggings: The Making of a Crow Warrior was published in 1967 by the Thomas Y. Crowell Company. It is not just an interesting narrative of a brave Crow warrior; it is a revealing account of the fascinating customs of the Crow people before they were restricted to an agrarian life style on reservations.

The selections which follow relate events in Two Leggings' boyhood which indicate the process of achieving manly status.

Bear White Child

As a boy I spent my evenings listening to the stories of our warriors and medicine men. I wanted to be just as brave and honored, and the following day would train myself that much harder, running and riding and playing war games with my friends.

When we were young, we did not speak; we listened to our Wise Ones. Sometimes we were told what to do and sometimes we learned through stories of true things that happened long ago. I will tell you the story of Bear White Child because it contains the most sacred instructions which can be given to a young man who hopes to become a chief. After it was told to me in those early days, I swore I would never be revengeful against my own people.

Early one night in leaf-falling season a full moon shone over a Crow village pitched along the ridge of a big coulee.[4] Old Man

---

[3] NAVAHO: also spelled "Navajo."

[4] COULEE (kōō'lē): deep gulch or ravine formed by rainstorms or melting snow.

Wolf, a Whistling Waters clan chief, walked through the camp calling certain men to his tepee for a smoke. When all were gathered, Old Man Wolf said that he wanted to smoke under grandmother moon. Buffalo robes were spread outside and the men sat in a half circle. After the pipe was passed, Old Man Wolf said that since game was scarce, they would move next day to where buffalo had been sighted nearby.

It was still dark face—the period just before dawn begins to color the eastern horizon—when the crier woke the camp, telling the women to prepare their men a good breakfast.

A Treacherous[5] clan chief, One Eye, also lived in this village. It was believed he could not be killed because he had been adopted by Bear Up Above, one of the most powerful supernatural persons. His clan members would abuse members of the Whistling Waters, knowing they were too afraid of One Eye to fight back, and One Eye himself often started feuds between the two clans.

A poor boy lived in this village, whose mother was his only living relative. But they belonged to the Whistling Waters clan; its members provided them with food and clothing.

Old Man Wolf had forgotten to invite One Eye to his meeting, and the clan leader brooded over this insult. He knew the boy was well liked by all the Whistling Waters, and planned his revenge.

The hunters left at dawn, followed by the skinners and women. As the sun rose, it became hotter. Everyone grew thirsty, and around the middle of the day they stopped at a small spring, where the water flowed cool and clear. After a short rest everyone went for one last drink.

The boy followed the older people, lying flat on his chest and putting his mouth into the water. Then One Eye, standing to one side, pressed his foot onto the boy's neck. All the people saw it but were afraid to do anything. One Eye talked loudly, pretending to give orders for the hunt. When bubbles came to the surface, One Eye took his foot away and joined his men.

Although the Whistling Waters members were angry, they were afraid of One Eye's power and of causing trouble in the tribe.

[5] TREACHEROUS: like the Whistling Waters, a particular clan of the Crow tribe.

Pulling the body from the spring, they laid it under a pine tree, covering it with a buffalo robe.

Late in the day they returned to bury him and were surprised to find the body gone. At first they thought some bear or mountain lion had dragged it off, but no tracks could be found. The next morning they carefully searched the surrounding hills, but discovered no signs.

Soon after being placed under the tree the boy had woken as if from a sleep. Instead of returning to his people he walked toward the mountains where he fasted and prayed. One night, at a place known as Bear Camp, he was told in a dream that Bear Up Above would adopt him in the new grass moon. All that winter the boy remained in the mountains, protected by the Without Fires. In the meantime he was almost forgotten in his village, although some felt that One Eye should be punished.

One day, as the boy was resting on a rock, a bird appeared and told him to be ready because Bear Up Above was going to adopt him. The bird said he should not be afraid; Bear Up Above would not hurt him.

As the boy remained on the rock, watching the setting sun, he noticed a black cloud, as if a storm were about to break. The cloud grew larger and more threatening. He felt strong gusts of wind and saw streaks of lightning. It began to rain very hard and he was afraid the large hailstones would kill him. As he ran for a place to hide, a voice told him not to fear, that he was about to be adopted.

The hail fell all around, but the boy was not touched. Again he looked in the direction the storm had come; a black cloud hung in the middle of the hail. The cloud's center began taking shape and he saw the head of Bear Up Above. At the moment the upper half of the bear's body appeared, the hail stopped. The bear sang a song as it reached down to embrace the boy. It lifted him into the air and when it finished singing, put him down.

After doing this four times, a fine-looking young man suddenly stood before the boy; he knew it was this same bear. The man said that he had adopted One Eye, but having seen One Eye's acts he had decided to take away his power. He had brought the boy back to life and had tested him. He said he knew how the boy had kept himself from the comforts of camp during the worst part of the year. He would reward him with the power he had once granted to One Eye. He gave the boy the name of Bear White Child.

The young man told Bear White Child that upon his return to the village he was to build four sweat lodges and invite everyone to enter them. He told the boy to offer a smoke to him there and said he would like this very much. Then the boy was to make One Eye miserable until the day came to kill him. For this he gave the boy bear sinew, a piece of which he was to throw into a fire. As it shriveled up, One Eye's body would also shrink until he died. The boy could kill all his enemies this way.

After telling Bear White Child where the camp had moved, the young man disappeared, leaving behind him a clear blue sky.

During the winter Bear White Child had grown into a young man. As he took the return trail, he felt strong and happy. He made himself a bow and arrows and on his way killed a deer, but ate very little. Reaching the outskirts of the village he sat down to rest. Then he rose, walked into the tepee of an old Whistling Waters clan member, and asked him to announce his return throughout the camp and to request his clan members to help him build four sweat lodges. The others in the tepee were surprised to see the boy grown up. After they had smoked, the old man announced the boy's return and repeated his request. The people thought he was crazy, but soon Bear White Child appeared, bringing in willow branches for the sweat lodges. One Eye was among the onlookers and was heard to say that the boy must have had some great dream and that he was glad to see him back. Actually, he was sure he had killed the boy and was afraid. Although One Eye flattered him in every way, Bear White Child ignored him.

After the sweat-lodge ceremony Bear White Child left the fourth lodge, lit his pipe, and offered the smoke to Bear Up Above. When a streak of lightning shot from the bowl to the sky, the people knew he must have some great power and were afraid of him. Then Bear White Child went to his mother's tepee where she was crying with joy at his return.

Nothing more happened until one night, in a dream, Bear White Child was told to fast on Long Mountain.

Early the next morning he told his mother he was leaving and to prepare him a good meal. Understanding that her son had some strong medicine power, she asked no questions. He had told a friend that he was fasting to the spirits, whose chief tepee was on Long Mountain, and his friend had asked to come. They climbed to the top and fixed their sleeping places. That night Bear Up Above appeared in the form of the fine-looking young man. He told Bear White Child that he had made him dream, and was appearing on the first night because he did not want to see Bear White Child suffer. Now was the time for Bear White Child to steal One Eye's youngest wife. Bear Up Above told him not to be afraid, for no one could harm him until he wanted to take Bear White Child back forever.

Bear White Child woke at daybreak and called to his friend that he was returning. When he told about his dream, his friend was glad because he hated One Eye.

After their return the crier announced that on the following day camp would move. That night Bear White Child stole One Eye's youngest wife, the prettiest girl in the tribe. Many young men wanted to marry her but had been afraid of One Eye's power. The news spread the next morning as the crier announced that camp would remain there because Bear White Child was to be married. The crier also told the women to make the new wife a deerskin dress covered with elk teeth. When someone asked One Eye what he was going to do, he said that both were young, that Bear White Child was a nice man and his wife good-looking. He said he could not blame him for stealing her and he thought they would be happy.

But One Eye sent her a message, warning that if she did not come to him, something bad would happen. Bear White Child told her that there was no need to be afraid; One Eye could do nothing. When she walked into One Eye's tepee, he was feeling good and said that he hoped she would be happy. As a wedding gift he gave her the pony that was her favorite and said he liked her husband. The people were surprised; they were sure One Eye would try to take some revenge.

As the season passed, Bear White Child stole One Eye's three remaining wives, and still One Eye did nothing. When autumn came, the Whistling Waters members urged Bear White Child to take his final revenge. Soon afterwards he asked his friends to build him a fire. When it was blazing, he threw in his piece of bear sinew, saying that it was One Eye's body. As the sinew twisted in the heat, One Eye, who was standing a few tepees away, suddenly fell groaning on his back. Everyone saw his body shrivel away and he died.

Then Bear White Child told the whole camp about his dream and said that he had thrown in all the sinew because he never wanted to use that revenge again.

FOR DISCUSSION

1. What is the most significant contrast between the characters of Bear White Child and One Eye? What function does the killing of One Eye serve, since the old man no longer appeared to be a threat after Bear White Child's return?

2. Why did Two Leggings think this story especially valuable for a young man who hoped to become a chief?

Achieving Manhood

One day in grass-growing moon, when I was about sixteen, Big Boat announced a raid. My brother wanted me to wait for a few summers, but it was time I made a name for myself. I found Big Boat preparing to leave with nine men and asked to go. He wanted to know what my brother thought. After telling him, I added that I could ride and shoot and run as well as anyone in our village.

Some of his men told him to let me come because I could carry the food, go for water, and collect firewood. I said I would be glad to be their helper.

Big Boat said I could come if my brother approved, and I ran back and begged until he finally agreed. At home I gathered a few pairs of moccasins, a buffalo robe, a new bow and twenty new arrows which my brother gave me, and an old knife traded from the Gros Ventre.[1] Long before dawn I was waiting in the dark outside Big Boat's tepee.

The sun was just rising as we left. We kept our faces north, crossing the Musselshell River and then the Big River. The first night out Big Boat chose a camping spot, and after ordering me to bring in some firewood, sat down to watch me. Then he told me to carry some water from a creek. When I had the fire going, he seemed satisfied.

Rolling up in my robe that night I thought that now I was poor and unknown, but soon people would be talking about me. And if I was not killed, some day I would become a chief with many honors and horses and property.

We traveled north for many days, even into the country of the Redcoats,[2] but saw no enemies. We wore out our spare moccasins and cut up our robes to make new ones. Finally we were killing prairie dogs to stay alive, and Big Boat decided to turn back.

After many days we reached the Gun River. It was too high to ford, so we tied driftwood poles together with rawhide, laid cross poles, and tied on our clothes. We fastened buckskin strings to each raft and held the ends in our teeth as we swam across with

---

[1] GROS VENTRE (grō vänt): the Atsina, a band of the Arapaho tribe (the French words mean "big belly").

[2] REDCOATS: British soldiers who were stationed in Canada at that time.

other poles under our arms. The current was so strong it carried us far down river, and when we reached the other bank, I was exhausted. But we had no time to rest and continued home.

As I was walking in the rear, someone called out that he saw a person and started running. As soon as the Blackfeet knew they had been discovered, they began yelling. All of them carried guns while we had only three. One of our men was shot in the arm; another, hit in the hand, shouted for us to stand or be killed. Throwing off my pack, I knelt and shot at the nearest Blackfeet, my arrow going through his neck and spinning him around. When I shot a second arrow into his arm, he tried to pull it out. I shot a third into his shoulder, and it bounced up and down as he ran back to his friends.

We entered a small coulee. Soon a Blackfeet looked over the ridge nearest us and asked in our language who we were. I shouted back that I was a Crow. He told us to go home because they had finished with us. One of their dogs walked close and I shot an arrow through its chest, yelling that if he came near, I would kill him like that.

A little later we watched them disappear into the hills. If they had been riding, we would probably have all been killed.

We had lost our robes and were nearly naked. We walked the rest of that day and long into the night before sleeping.

The next day we ran into a buffalo herd and then had enough meat for our trip back and hide to patch our moccasins. We were happy men a few days later when we walked into our village at the foot of Snowy Mountain.

There was much singing on our return, and I was mentioned as the only one who had wounded a Piegan. I had to tell my story to the friends and relatives who visited my brother's tepee. The two wounded men recovered, but the one man's hand was stiff for the rest of his life.

FOR DISCUSSION

1. Discuss the importance of bravery and endurance to the Crow people, using examples from the selection.

2. What have you learned about the personality of Two Leggings from "Bear White Child" and "Achieving Manhood"?

D. Chief Eagle

b. 1925

Born a descendant of the famous Sioux chiefs Red Cloud and Crazy Horse on the Rosebud Reservation in South Dakota, D. Chief Eagle was orphaned at an early age and brought up by elders of the tribe. A quick learner with great vitality, he became an important and influential member of his tribe. In 1967 he was named Chief of the Teton Sioux, an honor last conferred upon Red Cloud in 1868.

Chief Eagle is the author of four books of folklore and poetry, one of which is the historical novel Winter Count. In this book he relates the history of the Sioux conflicts with the white man from 1874 to 1890; the fictional hero, Turtleheart, is the adopted son of a chief and has as his comrades many famous Indian leaders —Sitting Bull, Red Cloud, and Crazy Horse among them.

The following selection from Winter Count tells about the great Sioux victory in 1876 at the Battle of Little Bighorn, also known as Custer's Last Stand. Eight years earlier the United States Government had told the Sioux that the Black Hills would belong to the Indians forever. This land had great religious significance for the Sioux, who believed it was the center of the world. Gold was discovered in the Black Hills, however, and war was declared when the Sioux refused to cede their land to the United States. Many Teton Sioux clans—Hunkpapa, Minneconjou, Ogalala,[1] Brulé, and Blackfoot—as well as Northern Cheyenne Indians converged forces on the Little Bighorn River and defeated General Custer in one of the most famous battles in American history.

---

[1] OGALALA: also spelled "Oglala."

Blood on the Little Bighorn

When the sound of gunfiring flailed the air like a thousand sticks breaking, Turtleheart's warriors were getting their horses ready to mount, desperation in their minds. They could not see the fighting, as the first attack was from up the Greasy Grass,[2] near the Hunkpapa village. The low hills obscured their vision.

Turtleheart sent three Cheyenne scouts toward the engagement to find out what was happening, but when they could catch no sight of the battle, they returned to crouch down behind a small bank within sight of Turtleheart.

Wild yells piercing the air announced the discovery of a second prong of the attack approaching the village of the Minneconjou. The waiting warriors could see their comrades ride to the battle with swinging tomahawks, clubs, and lances. While they watched the Cheyenne braves cross the river to meet the soldiers, Turtleheart was watching Sitting Bull moving about in all directions on top of a small hill. Astride a gray horse, he carried a crooked lance decorated with long banners, which he used for his silent commands.

Sitting Bull made an imposing sight on top of the hill, and he was closely watched by the chosen leaders at the battle scene. Interpreting his signals, they then relayed the desired information to the men in the battles.

Turning his attention to the battle, Turtleheart compared the Indians' attack to the actions of a school of fish. They rode to the attack in a broad sweeping curve to meet the Bluecoats,[3] who were approaching at a fast gallop.

Two riders were streaking toward Turtleheart's position, the froth flying from their horses' mouths. He recognized the warriors as Gall[4] and Strong Echo. As they came to a sliding halt, Gall shouted angrily, "I have made a fateful blunder. There are soldiers riding down the other side of the river toward the Cheyenne village, and that is where all of the women and children are. And the Cheyenne are going across the river."

[2] GREASY GRASS: the Little Bighorn area.
[3] BLUECOATS: soldiers of the United States Army.
[4] GALL: one of Sitting Bull's chief lieutenants.

A Cheyenne youth volunteered to go to the Ogalala village where the warriors were getting ready. "I will tell them we must brave a move to intercept the enemy before they reach my village."

"Move fast, boy," Gall commanded. "There is not much time."

"He has a long way to go. I hope he can make it," Strong Echo put in. Turtleheart echoed his thoughts.

Gall's voice was flat as he said, "When Strong Echo brought word that the soldiers to the east were going down to the area where our families are hidden, we wasted no time getting here. I could see them riding in columns of two across the open on the other side of the river, and I knew we must change our plans." He was visibly upset at this development.

"Look, across the river!" Turtleheart pointed toward Crazy Horse and his warriors riding fast across the slope.

"Hah, it is a move to cut off the enemy," Gall spoke in a tense manner as he slapped his horse into a full run.

Turtleheart motioned to four Minneconjous to follow him, and instructed them with a terse statement. "We are going to help our Cheyenne brothers draw the enemy."

He immediately set out with the four braves following. As they mounted the first hillock of ground, he and the four warriors gave loud war whoops and joined forces with four Cheyennes. There were now nine warriors on the way to attempt to decoy the soldiers from the lower end of the encampment. This was a very dangerous and desperate maneuver, one that could be fatal.

They were less than one hundred yards away when the soldiers caught sight of them. There was a noticeable slackening of pace as the troopers were undecided as to which group to follow. One of the Cheyenne warriors carefully aimed his gun and fired. The leader of the soldiers grabbed his shoulder, and the soldiers were no longer undecided.

The Indians turned and fled as the troops wheeled about and started after them. This was a gallant effort to draw the enemy, but it would be foolish and ineffectual to tarry longer. They raced for their very lives. Two of the Cheyenne were shot from their mounts. From the corner of his eye, Turtleheart saw two Minneconjous spin from their horses as rifle bullets struck them. These were no ordinary Bluecoats; they had an extraordinary skill with the rifle. The Indians were now pushing their horses to the limit while riding low alongside the horses' backs. All thoughts of heroics were gone. They had to reach the rest of the Indian forces or die.

There was sudden pandemonium as the concealed warriors left their place of hiding and charged the troopers. The air was filled with bloodcurdling screams intended to terrify the horses of the enemy and make them unmanageable. Turtleheart and his remaining companions turned their ponies and joined the flooding, screaming mass of painted Indian warriors.

Quickly scanning the area, Turtleheart could see the elite warriors under Crazy Horse's command sweeping in from the other side. The waters of the Little Bighorn turned red with blood in just minutes, as wounded and dead men and horses plunged into the river. The Bluecoats were utterly confused at the sudden turn of events and were looking for an avenue of escape.

At close quarters the long rifles were of no use, and the Indians were deadly with bows and arrows and lances. The horses reared frantically and threw many of the troopers. Horses which had been shot, bucked and screamed, and some dropped dead with riders still on their backs.

The battlefield was filled with dust and black smoke powder as the troops frantically made their way up the slope of a small hill. Soldiers and Indians were engaged in hand-to-hand combat. Horses were running back and forth in terror, adding to the confusion. Warriors in groups of two and three were rushing at the enemy to express their deeds of bravery by counting coup,[5] only to be killed by the soldiers for their reckless behavior. Many of the young and reckless braves crossed the death flights of their own comrades' arrows.

As the troopers began to dismount, Turtleheart could hear someone repeatedly ordering the Indian warriors to concentrate their fire on the still mounted soldiers.

Turtleheart and his men swept close to the hill where the soldiers were now concentrating, and he searched for the leading officer. He could not be seen; perhaps he was using his fallen horse as a breastwork. Circling to a stop, Turtleheart started to reload his gun. Looking around he was surprised to see that no man of the enemy was moving. The battlefield was quiet, except for the

---

[5] COUNTING COUP (co͞o): being the first to strike an enemy, often without a weapon.

loud yells of the Sioux and Cheyenne, and these sounds echoed in a strange way.

The full comprehension of what had happened turned the terrible war cries into resounding tones of victory and joy. Accompanying these sounds were those of sadness and despair as men and women searched and found fallen friends and relatives. The death wails of the women caused Turtleheart's flesh to crawl.

Rubbing his hand over his forehead, he jumped from his horse and stepped over the sprawling bodies of the soldiers as he ascended the hill. His body crouched over, he carefully and swiftly scrutinized the individual forms. Around him, the many saddles, blankets, white gloves, rifles, boots, and other items of clothing were being plundered by the victorious Indians. All of them were methodically scalping the dead and dying, so as to have hair to decorate their war shirts.

"Has anyone found the leader of the Bluecoats?" Gall's loud voice was unmistakable.

"Here. Over here!" someone answered. "He has yellow hair, and it is cut short."

"Yellow Hair," Turtleheart's body stiffened at the news.

"Loneman[6] was right when he said our enemy was commanded by the hated one!" Gall's voice commanded the attention of many of the nearby Indians, and they all rushed over to see for themselves if this was indeed the hated Custer.

Turtleheart and Gall were both running now and reached the spot where Broken Bow was excitedly gesturing. At his feet was the lifeless form of an officer with short yellow hair.

"Gall," said Turtleheart, "you are the rightful one to lay claim to this leader's weapons."

"No! No!" Broken Bow was emphatic in what he said. "I say this man shot himself. He destroyed his own life. To take anything of his is bad. It will bring bad things to you, your relatives, all of us. No, you cannot take anything."

"You saw him do this thing?" There was a puzzled expression on Gall's face as he questioned Broken Bow's statement.

Broken Bow let his eyes rest longingly on the pistols belonging to Yellow Hair before answering. "In the last of the battle, the

[6] LONEMAN: famous Sioux scout.

white handles on his short guns drew my eyes. He was crouched behind his dead horse and I was over there." He pointed to a few yards behind the slope. "I was about out of ammunition, so I lay there waiting for a soldier to die. When Yellow Hair stopped to reload his guns, I took advantage of his distracted attention and crawled closer. When he looked up and saw his forces crumbling all around him, there was terror on his face. He put a gun to his head with both hands and fired. When he did this thing, I knew I did not want his guns. I swear this is true."

Turtleheart looked at Yellow Hair and noticed that blood had run over his chin and mustache. He was lying on his back, eyes closed. His right hand, covered with blood, still clasped the left hand fingers which still held the gun.

Gall drove a war lance into the ground next to the body, then bent to strip the bloody coat from the leader. He hung the coat on the lance, saying, "It is evil medicine and a bad omen to take what belonged to one who takes his own life."

"As you say, Broken Bow," continued Gall, "this man has had his hair cut short. That is why we could not spot him in battle. We always knew him with long hair, like an Indian. That is all he ever did in common with us." Gall spat on the ground.

A lone horseman loped up to the group, and as he stopped, he said, "My relations, my victorious friends, press the eyelids of every soldier to make sure that none are among those who live." It was Sitting Bull who was issuing the orders.

"There is one over there who lives. If he is not seriously wounded, bring him here and tie him." Gall gave the commands.

The young soldier was dragged over and tied in spread-eagle fashion to await Sitting Bull's disposition. Although bleeding and in a somewhat dazed condition, the youth did not appear to be seriously wounded.

An elderly woman pushed her way through the gathering, and before anyone could stop her, she had mercilessly struck the soldier in the head with a tomahawk. He had been hit twice before she could be pulled away, but it was already too late, as the prisoner was dead.

"I had to avenge," she screamed. "I killed him to avenge my son who was just found dead." The words were hysterical, and as she was carried away by her relatives, she started a loud wail.

Sitting Bull strode over to ask, "Is he dead?"

Nodding heads affirmed the question.

"I need a live soldier to carry a message to Three Stars,[7] and now this one is no longer able to do this."

Near the body of Yellow Hair, Turtleheart saw a soldier move his head. Bending over the form, he turned the Bluecoat over and pressed his thumbs on the closed eyes. A strong moan escaped the lips.

"Come here; this one lives!" he shouted. "His head has been creased. Come help me get him to his feet."

"Make sure that nothing happens to this man," Sitting Bull roared. "I want him to carry a message. Protect him from the old women if you can." There was a note of derision in his voice.

Looking around, Sitting Bull seemed to be impatient. "I want Strong Echo. Find him. He can speak the enemy tongue."

Turtleheart was reviving the wounded soldier when Strong Echo came riding up on a cavalry horse. "You look for me?"

"Yes," said Sitting Bull. "You speak the tongue of the long knives, so tell this white warrior to ride to Three Stars with a message. He is to warn them that they are not to come into this area. If they do, they will meet the same fate as Yellow Hair and his men. Let him tell them that we will not meet with them until they have removed all of the white invaders from our hunting ground."

These words were greeted by loud cheers. Still shaky from his wound and surrounded by unfriendly painted faces, the young soldier was badly frightened. Deep down, Strong Echo felt sympathy for the man as he helped him mount a horse.

Struck on the rump by Strong Echo, the horse jumped and started running down the slope. The wild and loud jeers of the Indians echoed in the ears of both horse and rider and frightened them even more.

Strong Echo grunted and laughed, "The way he rides, I do not think I could catch him, even if I had to."

"Look, the horse has stumbled!" A cloud of dust marked the spot where the horse fell. The horse rose to his feet and galloped away, but the human form lay still.

[7] THREE STARS: General George Crook (1829–1890), famous Indian fighter of the United States Army.

Turtleheart raced his horse down the same path the soldier had taken, but warriors from the banks of the river were there first. "He is dead," they observed without emotion. "The fall broke his neck." They shrugged their shoulders and rode off.

Without dismounting, Turtleheart knew they were right, so he wheeled his pony around and rode back toward Sitting Bull.

On his way, he saw his grandmother standing by an arroyo,[8] so he detoured in her direction. She was watching other women loot the bodies and mutilate the naked forms. Her face brightened at the sight of him, and she came up to his horse. "I am so glad you are all right, my son. I prayed with my whole self for your safety."

Turtleheart jumped from his horse and took his grandmother by the shoulders. "You must dry your tears," he said. "I am safe and will be here to take care of you."

"I was standing here, afraid to go look for you. I feared I would find you among the dead. I am crying because I felt the joys of ancient times when I saw you."

"Come, grandmother, I will take you to the lodge and you can rest. You should not be here watching this. . . ."

"That does not disturb me so much, Turtleheart; I know that many mothers and wives have lost their loved ones to the guns of the invaders, so they must be allowed to destroy the ghost-spirits of the enemy."

"Just the same, grandmother, I am glad you are not out there doing as they are doing. And you must not watch."

Turtleheart looked out over the trampled hills and slopes. His heart was sick as he saw the desecration which was everywhere. "Grandmother, this morning that low hill was covered with tall grass waving in the wind, as the Holy Mystery intended. Look at it now, trampled and with the dead lying upon it. Man has defiled the goodness of Maka Ina.[9] Some of those dead out there were nothing but mere boys, and it is wrong for them to die. It does not matter whether they are friends and relatives, or white; this is wrong, all wrong. They should not have to die because of someone else. Come, grandmother, I do not want you here."

[8] ARROYO (ə·roi'ō): dry gulch, cut by a stream.
[9] MAKA INA: Mother Earth.

A truant curiosity lingered within his mind. Do the white women cry for their men who will never, ever return to their arms? In his heart he knew the answer, and the answer made him very sad.

FOR DISCUSSION

1. Compare the personalities of Gall and Turtleheart. What are Turtleheart's feelings as expressed in the last two paragraphs of the selection? What do you think Gall's reaction would have been as he looked over the battlefield?

2. From the material which you have read so far, list some conclusions you can draw about the Indians' feeling for life. Use examples from the selections to support your conclusions.

Black Elk

1863–1950

Black Elk's first-hand narration of the conflicts between the Sioux Indians and the white men during the nineteenth century is unique, expressing as much of the spiritual philosophy of the Sioux as it does of the history of this great tribe. Black Elk's life, in a sense, is a recapitulation of that history: he lived through the Battle of Little Bighorn; he witnessed numerous conferences between the whites and the Sioux; and he even lived long enough to become one of the several Sioux who performed with Buffalo Bill's Wild West Show for Queen Victoria of England, who said, "All over the world I have seen all kinds of people; but today I have seen the best-looking people I know."

Yet for all these worldly accomplishments, Black Elk considered the earth "a world of darkness and many shadows"; he preferred the Other World, the world of the spirit, where beauty and truth reigned eternal. When he was nine years old, he experienced a great vision in which the "Six Grandfathers"—the West, the East, the North, the South, the Sky, and the Earth—revealed to him the future of his people and his personal responsibility to that destiny. Throughout his life this vision influenced and shaped his perceptions; and Black Elk was a holy man among the Sioux.

The last few years of his life were relatively calm in comparison to those of his youth. In 1930 he met noted author John G. Neihardt, who he believed had been preordained to record his life history. "He has been sent to learn what I know, and I will teach him." For Black Elk felt that before his death, he must "save his Great Vision for men." Black Elk Speaks, as told through John G. Neihardt, was published in 1932 by William Morrow & Company and was republished in 1961 by the University of Nebraska Press.

The following selection from Black Elk Speaks *describes the killing of the last of the great Sioux war chiefs, Crazy Horse. After the Sioux victory at the Battle of Little Bighorn, the United States Army was determined either to place all Indians on reservations, or, if they refused to go, to destroy them. Red Cloud and Spotted Tail acquiesced to the whites' demands and entered reservations; Sitting Bull fled with his clan to Canada. By 1877 the only chief left free was Crazy Horse, proud but starving along with his clan of some nine hundred Ogalalas. Black Elk was then a fourteen-year-old boy in Crazy Horse's camp.*

The Killing of Crazy Horse

One night early in the Moon When the Calf Grows Hair (September) we broke camp there at Red Cloud Agency without making any noise, and started. My father told me we were going to Spotted Tail's camp, but he did not tell me why until later. We traveled most of the night and then we camped.

But when we were moving again next day, a band of Red Cloud's people overtook us and said there would be bad trouble if we did not come back right away. Some of us turned around then and went back, and soldiers sent the others back a little later; but Crazy Horse went on to his uncle's camp.

After what happened, my father told me why Crazy Horse had done this. He was afraid somebody might start trouble down there where all the soldiers were, and the Wasichus[1] had taken our guns away from us, so that we could do nothing if there was bad trouble. The Wasichus had made Spotted Tail head chief of all the Lakotas[2] because he would do what they wanted, and Crazy Horse thought we might be safer there with his uncle. Afterwards, the Hang-

---

[1] WASICHUS: term designating white men, though having no reference to their color.

[2] LAKOTAS: Teton Sioux's name for themselves; the Santee Sioux referred to themselves as Dakotas.

Around-the-Fort people[3] said that he was getting ready to tie up his horse's tail[4] again and make war on the Wasichus. How could he do that when we had no guns and could not get any? It was a story the Wasichus told, and their tongues were forked when they told it. Our people believe they did what they did because he was a great man and they could not kill him in battle and he would not make himself over into a Wasichu, as Spotted Tail and the others did. That summer, my father told me, the Wasichus wanted him to go to Washington with Red Cloud and Spotted Tail and others to see the Great Father there; but he would not go. He told them that he did not need to go looking for his Great Father. He said: "My Father is with me, and there is no Great Father between me and the Great Spirit."

In the evening of the next day after we got back to Red Cloud's Agency, some soldiers came there bringing Crazy Horse with them. He was riding his horse alone a little way ahead. They did not stay there long, but rode on over to the Soldiers' Town,[5] and my father and I went along with many others to see what they were going to do.

When we got over there, we could not see Crazy Horse, because there were soldiers and Lakota policemen all around where he was and people crowding outside.

In just a little while I could feel that something very bad was happening in there, and everybody was excited all at once, and you could hear voices buzzing all around. Then I heard a loud cry in our own language, and it said: "Don't touch me! I am Crazy Horse!" And suddenly something went through all the people there like a big wind that strikes many trees all at once. Somebody in there yelled something else, but everybody around me was asking or telling everybody what had happened, and I heard that Crazy Horse was killed, that he was sick, that he was hurt; and I was frightened, because everything felt the way it did that day when we were going up to kill on the Greasy Grass, and it seemed we might all begin fighting right away.

[3] HANG . . . PEOPLE: derisive name applied to Spotted Tail's Brulé Sioux by other Sioux clans.
[4] TIE . . . TAIL: Sioux expression for preparing to make war.
[5] SOLDIER'S TOWN: Fort Robinson.

Then everything got quiet, and everybody seemed to be waiting for something. Then the people began to break up and move around, and I heard that Crazy Horse had just taken sick and maybe he would be all right soon.

But it was not long until we all knew what had happened in there, because some of the people saw it happen, and I will tell you how it was.

They told Crazy Horse they would not harm him if he would go to the Soldiers' Town and have a talk with the Wasichu chief there. But they lied. They did not take him to the chief for a talk They took him to the little prison with iron bars on the windows, for they had planned to get rid of him. And when he saw what they were doing, he turned around and took a knife out of his robe and started out against all those soldiers. Then Little Big Man, who had been his friend and was the one who told us boys that we were brave before my first fight when we attacked the wagons on War Bonnet Creek, took hold of Crazy Horse from behind and tried to get the knife away. And while they were struggling, a soldier ran a bayonet into Crazy Horse from one side at the back and he fell down and began to die. Then they picked him up and carried him into the soldier chief's office. The soldiers stood all around there and would not let anybody in and made the people go away. My father and I went back to our camp at Red Cloud Agency.

That night I heard mourning somewhere, and then there was more and more mourning, until it was all over the camp.

Crazy Horse was dead. He was brave and good and wise. He never wanted anything but to save his people, and he fought the Wasichus only when they came to kill us in our own country. He was only thirty years old. They could not kill him in battle. They had to lie to him and kill him that way.

I cried all night, and so did my father.

When it was day, Crazy Horse's father and mother brought him over to our camp in a wagon. Then they put him in a box, and I heard that they had to cut him in two because the box was not long enough. They fastened the box on a pony drag and went away alone toward the east and north. I saw the two old people going away alone with their son's body. Nobody followed them. They went all alone, and I can see them going yet. The horse that pulled the pony drag was a buckskin. Crazy Horse's father had a white-faced bay with white hind legs. His mother had a brown mare with a bay colt.

The old people never would tell where they took the body of their son. Nobody knows today where he lies, for the old people are dead too. Many have talked about the place, and some have said they knew where it was and would not tell, and many think it is somewhere on Bear Creek in the Badlands. I know one thing, and this is it. The old people came with the body right down Pepper Creek which is just a little way south across the hill from where we are.[6] There were two hunters who were hunting along the creek there, and they saw two old people coming with a pony drag, and when they told my father about this, they said a buck-skin was pulling the drag that had a box on it; that the old man rode a white-faced bay with white hind legs and the old woman rode a brown mare with a bay colt. These hunters saw the old people coming down Pepper Creek, and later on they saw the old people again on White Horse Creek which is just a little way down Pepper Creek from where they were before. And the hunters said the box was not on the drag any more. So I think that maybe they hid the body somewhere on Pepper Creek over there because the hunters had seen them, and maybe they went back again at night and took the box away into the Badlands. But Crazy Horse might be lying over there just a little way from us right now on Pepper Creek across that hill yonder. I do not know.

It does not matter where his body lies, for it is grass; but where his spirit is, it will be good to be.

[6] HILL . . . ARE: Black Elk's log cabin on Pine Ridge Reservation.

FOR DISCUSSION

1. Describe the personality of Crazy Horse as depicted by Black Elk. Do you learn anything of Black Elk's character as well? Discuss.

2. In speaking of the white men who negotiated with the Sioux, Black Elk said, "It was a story the Wasichus told, and their tongues were forked when they told it." This statement is often attributed to Indians in their evaluation of white men. What does it mean?

The Indians' living conditions deteriorated steadily during the 1880s. Most Indians were confined to reservations, and hunting was no longer permitted; even if it had been, almost all the buffalo had been slaughtered by the white man. These first few years of life on reservations were especially hard. Many Indians died—of malnutrition, of disease, and often of despair.

Beginning in 1888, a revivalist Indian cult, inspired by a Paiute medicine man named Wovoka, swept through the Plains Indians. Wovoka's preachings, later to be known as the Ghost Dance religion, were a combination of traditional Indian religious practice and Christianity. Wovoka believed that God had ordained him to tell the people that if they were good and loved one another, if they lived in peace with the white man, and if they performed the dance which he would teach them, then they would be reunited with their friends and relations in the Other World; and the happy days of the past, including an infinite number of buffalo, would once again be a reality. This messianic belief found fertile soil among the Plains Indians, and within two years it had spread from Nevada through Nebraska.

The United States Government, not understanding the Ghost Dance faith, grew nervous and tried to suppress it. The Indians, not feeling that they were practicing anything harmful, refused to stop. Tensions grew on both sides and climaxed in battle at "The Butchering at Wounded Knee" on December 29, 1890. Black Elk, then twenty-seven years old, witnessed this event.

The Butchering at Wounded Knee

That evening before it happened, I went into Pine Ridge and heard these things,[1] and while I was there, soldiers started for where the Big Foots were. These made about five hundred soldiers that were

[1] HEARD ... THINGS: Members of the band of Chief Big Foot, a Hunkpapa Sioux, fled from Cheyenne River Reservation after the killing of Sitting Bull in December, 1890, and attempted to join other Sioux in the Badlands.

there next morning. When I saw them starting, I felt that something terrible was going to happen. That night I could hardly sleep at all. I walked around most of the night.

In the morning I went out after my horses, and while I was out, I heard shooting off toward the east, and I knew from the sound that it must be wagon-guns (cannon) going off. The sounds went right through my body, and I felt that something terrible would happen.

When I reached camp with the horses, a man rode up to me and said: "Hey-hey-hey! The people that are coming are fired on! I know it!"

I saddled up my buckskin and put on my sacred shirt. It was one I had made to be worn by no one but myself. It had a spotted eagle outstretched on the back of it, and the daybreak star was on the left shoulder, because when facing south that shoulder is toward the east. Across the breast, from the left shoulder to the right hip, was the flaming rainbow, and there was another rainbow around the neck, like a necklace, with a star at the bottom. At each shoulder, elbow, and wrist was an eagle feather; and over the whole shirt were red streaks of lightning. You will see that this was from my great vision, and you will know how it protected me that day.

I painted my face all red, and in my hair I put one eagle feather for the One Above.

It did not take me long to get ready, for I could still hear the shooting over there.

I started out alone on the old road that ran across the hills to Wounded Knee. I had no gun. I carried only the sacred bow of the west[2] that I had seen in my great vision. I had gone only a little way when a band of young men came galloping after me. The first two who came up were Loves War and Iron Wasichu. I asked what they were going to do, and they said they were just going to see where the shooting was. Then others were coming up, and some older men.

We rode fast, and there were about twenty of us now. The shooting was getting louder. A horseback from over there came galloping very fast toward us, and he said: "Hey-hey-hey! They

[2] SACRED . . . WEST: i.e., the power to destroy, given to Black Elk by the Grandfather of the West.

have murdered them!" Then he whipped his horse and rode away faster toward Pine Ridge.

In a little while we had come to the top of the ridge where, looking to the east, you can see for the first time the monument and the burying ground on the little hill where the church is. That is where the terrible thing started. Just south of the burying ground on the little hill a deep dry gulch runs about east and west, very crooked, and it rises westward to nearly the top of the ridge where we were. It had no name, but the Wasichus sometimes call it Battle Creek now. We stopped on the ridge not far from the head of the dry gulch. Wagon-guns were still going off over there on the little hill, and they were going off again where they hit along the gulch. There was much shooting down yonder, and there were many cries, and we could see cavalrymen scattered over the hills ahead of us. Cavalrymen were riding along the gulch and shooting into it, where the women and children were running away and trying to hide in the gullies and the stunted pines.

A little way ahead of us, just below the head of the dry gulch, there were some women and children who were huddled under a clay bank, and some cavalrymen were there pointing guns at them.

We stopped back behind the ridge, and I said to the others: "Take courage. These are our relatives. We will try to get them back." Then we all sang a song which went like this:

"A thunder being nation I am, I have said.
A thunder being nation I am, I have said.
You shall live.
You shall live.
You shall live.
You shall live."

Then I rode over the ridge and the others after me, and we were crying: "Take courage! It is time to fight!" The soldiers who were guarding our relatives shot at us and then ran away fast, and some more cavalrymen on the other side of the gulch did too. We got our relatives and sent them across the ridge to the northwest where they would be safe.

I had no gun, and when we were charging, I just held the sacred bow out in front of me with my right hand. The bullets did not hit us at all.

We found a little baby lying all alone near the head of the gulch. I could not pick her up just then, but I got her later and some of my people adopted her. I just wrapped her up tighter in a shawl that was around her and left her there. It was a safe place, and I had other work to do.

The soldiers had run eastward over the hills where there were some more soldiers, and they were off their horses and lying down. I told the others to stay back, and I charged upon them holding the sacred bow out toward them with my right hand. They all shot at me, and I could hear bullets all around me, but I ran my horse right close to them, and then swung around. Some soldiers across the gulch began shooting at me too, but I got back to the others and was not hurt at all.

By now many other Lakotas, who had heard the shooting, were coming up from Pine Ridge, and we all charged on the soldiers. They ran eastward toward where the trouble began. We followed down along the dry gulch, and what we saw was terrible. Dead and wounded women and children and little babies were scattered all along there where they had been trying to run away. The soldiers had followed along the gulch, as they ran, and murdered them in there. Sometimes they were in heaps because they had huddled together, and some were scattered all along. Sometimes bunches of them had been killed and torn to pieces where the wagon-guns hit them. I saw a little baby trying to suck its mother, but she was bloody and dead.

There were two little boys at one place in this gulch. They had guns and they had been killing soldiers all by themselves. We could see the soldiers they had killed. The boys were all alone there, and they were not hurt. These were very brave little boys.

When we drove the soldiers back, they dug themselves in, and we were not enough people to drive them out from there. In the evening they marched off up Wounded Knee Creek, and then we saw all that they had done there.

Men and women and children were heaped and scattered all over the flat at the bottom of the little hill where the soldiers had their wagon-guns, and westward up the dry gulch all the way to the high ridge, the dead women and children and babies were scattered.

When I saw this, I wished that I had died too, but I was not sorry for the women and children. It was better for them to be happy in the other world, and I wanted to be there too. But before I went there, I wanted to have revenge. I thought there might be a day, and we should have revenge.

After the soldiers marched away, I heard from my friend, Dog Chief, how the trouble started, and he was right there by Yellow Bird when it happened. This is the way it was:

In the morning the soldiers began to take all the guns away from the Big Foots, who were camped in the flat below the little hill where the monument and burying ground are now. The people had stacked most of their guns, and even their knives, by the tepee where Big Foot was lying sick. Soldiers were on the little hill and all around, and there were soldiers across the dry gulch to the south and over east along Wounded Knee Creek too. The people were nearly surrounded, and the wagon-guns were pointing at them.

Some had not yet given up their guns, and so the soldiers were searching all the tepees, throwing things around and poking into everything. There was a man called Yellow Bird, and he and another man were standing in front of the tepee where Big Foot was lying sick. They had white sheets around and over them, with eyeholes to look through, and they had guns under these. An officer came to search them. He took the other man's gun, and then started to take Yellow Bird's. But Yellow Bird would not let go. He wrestled with the officer, and while they were wrestling, the gun went off and killed the officer. Wasichus and some others have said he meant to do this, but Dog Chief was standing right there, and he told me it was not so. As soon as the gun went off, Dog Chief told me, an officer shot and killed Big Foot who was lying sick inside the tepee.

Then suddenly nobody knew what was happening, except that the soldiers were all shooting and the wagon-guns began going off right in among the people.

Many were shot down right there. The women and children ran into the gulch and up west, dropping all the time, for the soldiers shot them as they ran. There were only about a hundred warriors and there were nearly five hundred soldiers. The warriors rushed to where they had piled their guns and knives. They fought soldiers with only their hands until they got their guns.

Dog Chief saw Yellow Bird run into a tepee with his gun, and from there he killed soldiers until the tepee caught fire. Then he died full of bullets.

It was a good winter day when all this happened. The sun was shining. But after the soldiers marched away from their dirty work, a heavy snow began to fall. The wind came up in the night. There was a big blizzard, and it grew very cold. The snow drifted deep in the crooked gulch, and it was one long grave of butchered women and children and babies, who had never done any harm and were only trying to run away.

And so it was all over.

I did not know then how much was ended. When I look back now from this high hill of my old age, I can still see the butchered women and children lying heaped and scattered all along the crooked gulch as plain as when I saw them with eyes still young. And I can see that something else died there in the bloody mud, and was buried in the blizzard. A people's dream died there. It was a beautiful dream.

And I, to whom so great a vision was given in my youth—you see me now a pitiful old man who has done nothing, for the nation's hoop is broken and scattered. There is no center any longer, and the sacred tree is dead.

FOR DISCUSSION

1. In describing his part at the Battle of Wounded Knee, Black Elk said that "the bullets did not hit us at all." Can you explain this phenomenon? Was it a matter of luck, or do you think it is possible that Black Elk had supernatural powers? Defend your answer.

2. What does Black Elk mean by "A people's dream died there. It was a beautiful dream"?

3. This battle has historically been called the Battle of Wounded Knee; the Indians usually refer to it as the Massacre of the Big Foot Band. Which title do you think is more apt? Discuss.

Charles A. Eastman

1858–1939

One of the first Indians to assume the white man's life style, Charles Alexander Eastman became a noted author as well as a physician. Born near Redwood Falls, Minnesota, Eastman was a Santee Sioux whose name, until he began attending school, was Ohíyesa, "the winner." Greatly influenced by his father, who had accepted Christianity and the civilization of the white man, Ohíyesa attended the mission school at Santee, Nebraska, and then Beloit College in Wisconsin. He was graduated from Dartmouth College in 1887, and in 1890 he received his M.D. from Boston University School of Medicine.

For many years Dr. Eastman worked at Indian agencies as Government physician and as traveling secretary of the Young Men's Christian Association. Much of his life was devoted toward creating greater understanding of the respective cultures of the Indians and white men.

Indian Boyhood, Dr. Eastman's first book, was published in 1902. Red Hunters and the Animal People followed in 1904. "On the White Man's Trail," the selection reprinted in this book, is from his autobiography From the Deep Woods to Civilization, published in 1916. This selection relates Ohíyesa's introduction to white civilization as he travels to and attends the mission school in Santee.

49

On the White Man's Trail

It was in the fall of 1874 that I started from Flandreau, then only an Indian settlement, with a good neighbor of ours, Peter, on his way to Santee. There were only a dozen houses or so at Sioux Falls, and the whole country was practically uninhabited, when we embarked in a homemade prairie schooner[1] on that bright September morning.

I had still my Hudson Bay flintlock gun, which I had brought down with me from Canada the year before. I took that old companion, with my shot-pouch and a well-filled powder horn. All I had besides was a blanket and an extra shirt. I wore my hunting suit, which was a compromise between Indian attire and a frontiersman's outfit. I was about sixteen years old and small of my age.

"Remember, my boy, it is the same as if I sent you on your first warpath. I shall expect you to conquer," was my father's farewell. My good grandmother, who had brought me up as a motherless child, bestowed upon me her blessing. "Always remember," said she, "that the Great Mystery is good; evil can come only from ourselves!" Thus I parted with my first teacher—the woman who taught me to pray!

Our first night out was at Hole-in-the-Hill, one of the most picturesque spots in the valley. Here I brought in a doe, which I had come upon in the tall grass of the river bottom. Peter shot several ducks, and we had a good supper. It seemed to me more like one of our regular fall hunts than like going away to school.

After supper I said, "I am going to set some of your traps, uncle."[2]

"And I will go with you," replied Peter. "But before we go, we must have our prayer," and he took out his Bible and hymnbook printed in the Indian tongue.

It was all odd enough to me, for although my father did the same, I had not yet become thoroughly used to such things. Nevertheless, it was the new era for the Indian; and while we were still

[1] PRAIRIE SCHOONER: lightweight, canvas-covered wagon.
[2] UNCLE: affectionate term applied to an older man.

seated on the ground around the central fire of the Sioux tepee and had just finished our repast of wild game, Peter read from the good book and performed the devotional exercises of his tepee home with quite as much zeal as if he were within four walls and surrounded by civilized things. I was very much impressed when this primitive Christian prayed that I might succeed in my new undertaking.

The next morning was frosty, and after an early breakfast we hurried to our traps. I got two fine minks and a beaver for my trouble, while Peter came home smiling with two otters and three beaver. I saw that he had something on his mind, but like a true Indian, I held my peace. At last he broke the news to me—he had changed his mind about going to Santee agency!

I did not blame him—it was hard to leave such a trapper's paradise as this, alive with signs of otter, mink, and beaver. I said nothing but thought swiftly. The temptation was strong to remain and trap too. That would please my grandmother; and I will confess here that no lover is more keen to do the right thing for the loved one than I was at that time to please my old grandmother.

The thought of my father's wish kept me on my true course. Leaving my gun with Peter, I took my blanket on my back and started for the Missouri on foot.

"Tell my father," I said, "that I shall not return until I finish my warpath."

But the voice of the waterfall, near what is now the city of Sioux Falls, sounded like the spirits of woods and water crying for their lost playmate, and I thought for a moment of turning back to Canada, there to regain my freedom and wild life. Still, I had sent word to my father that this warpath should be completed, and I remembered how he had said that if I did not return, he would shed proud tears.

About this time I did some of the hardest thinking that I have ever done in my life. All day I traveled and did not see anyone until, late in the afternoon, descending into the valley of a stream, I came suddenly upon a solitary farmhouse of sod and was met by a white man—a man with much hair on his face.

I was hungry and thirsty as a moose in burned timber. I had some money that my father had given me—I hardly knew the different denominations; so I showed the man all of it and told him by signs that he might take what he pleased if only he would let me have something to eat and a little food to carry with me. As for lodging, I would not have slept in his house if he had promised me a war bonnet!

While he was cordial—at any rate, after I exhibited my money—there was something about his manner that did not put me at my ease, and my wild instincts told me to keep an eye on him. But I was not alone in this policy, for his flock of four daughters and a son nearly put their necks out of joint in following my modest, shy movements.

When they invited me to sit down with them at the table, I felt uncomfortable, but hunger was stronger than my fears and modesty. The climax came when I took my seat on a rickety stool between the big, hairy man and one of his well-grown daughters. I felt not unlike a young blue heron just leaving the nest to partake of his first meal on an unsafe, swinging branch. I was entirely uncertain of my perch.

All at once, without warning, the man struck the table with the butt of his knife with such force that I jumped and was within an ace of giving a war whoop. In spite of their taking a firm hold of the homemade table to keep it steady, the dishes were quivering, and the young ladies no longer able to maintain their composure. Severe glances from mother and father soon brought us calm, when it appeared that the blow on the table was merely a signal for quiet before saying grace. I pulled myself in, much as a turtle would do, and possibly it should be credited to the stoicism of my race that I scarcely ever ate a heartier meal.

After supper I got up and held out to the farmer nearly all the money I had. I did not care whether he took it all or not. I was grateful for the food, and money had no such hold on my mind as it has gained since. To my astonishment, he simply smiled, shook his head, and stroked his shaggy beard.

I was invited to join the family in the sod-house parlor, but owing to the severe nerve shocks that I had experienced at the supper table, I respectfully declined and betook myself to the bank of the stream nearby, where I sat down to meditate. Presently there pealed forth a peculiar, weird music and the words of a strange song. It was music from a melodeon,[3] but I did not then know

---

[3] MELODEON: small reed organ.

what that was; and the tune was "Nearer, My God, to Thee." Strange as it sounded to me, I felt that there was something sooth- ing and gentle about the music and the voices.

After a while curiosity led me back to the sod house, and I saw for the first time how the white woman pumps so much air into a box that when she presses on the top boards, it howls convul- sively. I forgot my bashfulness so far as to listen openly and enjoy the operation, wondering much how the white man puts a pair of lungs into a box, which is furnished with a whole set of black and white teeth, and when he sings to it, it appears to answer him.

Presently I walked over to a shed where the farmer seemed to be very busy with his son, earnestly hammering something with all their might in the midst of glowing fire and sparks. He had an old breaking plow which he was putting into shape on his rude forge. With sleeves rolled up, face and hands blackened and streaming with sweat, I thought he looked not unlike a successful warrior just returned from the field of battle. His powerful muscles and the manly way in which he handled the iron impressed me tremendously. "I shall learn that profession if ever I reach the school and learn the white man's way," I thought.

I thanked the good man for his kind invitation to sleep within the sod walls with all his family, but signed to him that I preferred to sleep out-of-doors. I could see some distrust in his eyes, for his horses were in the open stable; and at that my temper rose, but I managed to control it. He had been kind to me, and no Indian will break the law of hospitality unless he has lost all the trails of his people. The man looked me over again carefully and ap- peared satisfied; and I rolled myself up in my blanket among the willows, but every star that night seemed to be bent upon telling the story of the white man.

I slept little, and early the next morning I was awakened by the barking of the farmer's collie and the laughter of his daughters. I got up and came to the house. Breakfast was nearly ready, and every member of the family was on hand. After breakfast I once more offered my money but was refused. I was glad. Then and there I loved civilization and renounced my wild life.

I took up my blanket and continued on my journey, which for three days was a lonely one. I had nothing with which to kill any game, so I stopped now and then at a sod house for food. When I reached the back hills of the Missouri, there lay before me a long slope leading to the river bottom, and upon the broad flat, as far as my eyes could reach, lay farmhouses and farms. Ah! I thought, this is the way of civilization, the basis upon which it rests! I desired to know that life.

Thirty miles from the school I met Dr. Riggs on the road, coming to the town of Yankton, and received some encouraging words from him, for he spoke the Sioux language very well. A little further on I met the Indian agent, Major Sears, a Quaker, and he, too, gave me a word of encouragement when he learned that I had walked a hundred and fifty miles to school. My older brother John, who was then assistant teacher and studying under Dr. Riggs, met me at the school and introduced me to my new life.

The bell of the old chapel at Santee summoned the pupils to class. Our principal read aloud from a large book and offered prayer. Although he conducted devotional exercises in the Sioux language, the subject matter was still strange, and the names he used were unintelligible to me. *Jesus* and *Jehovah* fell upon my ears as mere meaningless sounds.

I understood that he was praying to the "Great Mystery" that the work of the day might be blessed and their labor be fruitful. A cold sweat came out upon me as I heard him ask the "Great Mystery" to be with us in that day's work in that school building. I thought it was too much to ask of him. I had been taught that the Supreme Being is only concerned with spirits, and that when one wishes to commune with him in nature, he must be in a spiritual attitude and must retire from human sound or influence, alone in the wilderness. Here for the first time I heard him addressed openly in the presence of a house full of young men and young girls!

All the scholars were ordered to various rooms under different instructors, and I was left in the chapel with another long-haired young man. He was a Mandan from Fort Berthold—one of our ancient enemies. Not more than two years before that time my uncle had been on the warpath against this tribe and had brought home two Mandan scalps. He, too, was a new scholar and looked as if he were about to come before the judge to receive his sentence. My heart at once went out to him, although the other pupils were all of my own tribe, the Sioux. I noticed that he had beautiful long hair arranged in two plaits, and in spite of his sad face he was noble-looking and appeared to great advantage, I thought, in contrast with the other pupils, whose hair was cut short and their garments not becoming to them at all. This boy, Alfred Mandan, became a very good friend of mine.

Dr. Riggs took me in hand and told me the rules of the school and what was expected of us. There was the chapel, which was used as a church every Sunday and as a schoolhouse on weekdays. There was the Dakota Home for the girls' dormitory—a small, square frame building—and for the boys a long log house some two hundred yards from the chapel under the large cottonwood trees.

Dr. Riggs said that I need not study that first day, but could fill up the big bag he brought me with straw from the straw pile back of his barn. I carried it over to the log cabin, where the doctor was before me and had provided a bunk or framework for my bed. I filled a smaller bag for a pillow, and having received the sheets and blankets, I made my first white man's bed under his supervision. When it was done, it looked clean and dignified enough for anyone, I thought.

He said that I must make it every morning like that before going to school. "And for your wash, there is a tin basin or two on a bench just outside of the door, by the water barrels." And so it was. We had three barrels of Missouri River water, which we ourselves filled up every week, for we boys had to furnish our own water and wood and were detailed in pairs for this work.

Dr. Riggs supplied axes for the woodchoppers, and barrels and pails for the water carriers, also a yoke of large and gentle white oxen and a lumber wagon. It seems to me that I never was better acquainted with two animals than with these two! I have done some of my solemnest thinking behind them. The Missouri River was about two miles from our log house, with a wide stretch of bottom land intervening, partly cottonwood timber and partly open meadow with tall grass. I could take a nap or dance a war dance, if I cared to do so, while they were carrying me to wood or to water.

Dr. Riggs gave me a little English primer to study, also one or two books in the Dakota language, which I had learned to read in the day school. There was a translation of the Psalms and of *The Pilgrim's Progress*. I must confess that at that time I would have preferred one of grandmother's evening stories or my uncle's account of his day's experiences in the chase. I thought it was the dullest hunting I had ever known!

Toward evening a company of three young men arrived from up the river—to all appearance full-fledged warriors. Ah, it was good to see the handsome white, blue, and red blankets worn by these stately Sioux youths! I had not worn one since my return from Canada. My brother got me a suit of clothes, and had someone cut my hair, which was already over my ears, as it had not been touched since the year before. I felt like a wild goose with its wings clipped.

Next morning the day pupils emerged in every direction from the woods and deep ravines where the Indians had made their temporary homes, while we, the log-cabin boarders, came out in Indian file. The chapel bell was tolling as we reached the yard, when my attention was attracted to a pretty lass standing with her parents and Dr. Riggs near the Dakota Home. Then they separated and the father and mother came toward us, leaving the doctor and the pretty Dakota maiden standing still. All at once the girl began to run toward her parents, screaming pitifully.

"Oh, I cannot, I cannot stay in the white man's house! I'll die, I'll die! Mamma! Mamma!"

The parents stopped and reasoned with the girl, but it was of no use. Then I saw them leading her back to the Dakota Home, in spite of her pleading and begging. The scene made my blood boil, and I suppressed with difficulty a strong desire to go to her aid.

How well I remember the first time we were called upon to recite! In the same primer class were Eagle-Crane, Kite, and their compatriot from up the river. For a whole week we youthful warriors were held up and harassed with words of three letters. Like raspberry bushes in the path, they tore, bled, and sweated us—those little words *rat, cat,* and so forth—until not a semblance of our native dignity and self-respect was left. And we were of just the age when the Indian youth is most on his dignity! Imagine the same fellows turned loose against Custer or Harney[4] with anything like equal numbers and weapons, and those tried generals would

[4] HARNEY: General William S. Harney (1800–1889), active in Indian conflicts at that time.

feel like boys! We had been bred and trained to those things; but when we found ourselves within four walls and set to pick out words of three letters, we were like novices upon snowshoes—often flat on the ground.

I hardly think I was ever tired in my life until those first days of boarding school. All day things seemed to come and pass with a wearisome regularity, like walking railway ties—the step was too short for me. At times I felt something of the fascination of the new life, and again there would arise in me a dogged resistance, and a voice seemed to be saying, "It is cowardly to depart from the old things!"

Aside from repeating and spelling words, we had to count and add imaginary amounts. We never had had any money to count, nor potatoes, nor turnips, nor bricks. Why, we valued nothing except honor; that cannot be purchased! It seemed now that everything must be measured in time or money or distance. And when the teacher placed before us a painted globe and said that our world was like that—that upon such a thing our forefathers had roamed and hunted for untold ages, as it whirled and danced around the sun in space—I felt that my foothold was deserting me. All my savage training and philosophy was in the air, if these things were true.

Later on, when Dr. Riggs explained to us the industries of the white man, his thrift and forethought, we could see the reasonableness of it all. Economy is the able assistant of labor, and the two together produce great results. The systems and methods of business were of great interest to us, and especially the adoption of a medium of exchange.

The doctor's own personality impressed us deeply, and his words of counsel and daily prayers, strange to us at first, in time found root in our minds. Next to my own father, this man did more than perhaps any other to make it possible for me to grasp the principles of true civilization. He also strengthened and developed in me that native strong ambition to win out, by sticking to whatever I might undertake. Associated with him was another man who influenced me powerfully toward Christian living. This was the Reverend Doctor John P. Williamson, the pioneer Presbyterian missionary. The world seemed gradually to unfold before me, and the desire to know all that the white man knows was the tremendous and prevailing thought in me and was constantly growing upon me more and more.

My father wrote to me in the Dakota language for my encouragement. Dr. Riggs had told him that I was not afraid of books or of work, but rather determined to profit by them. "My son," he wrote, "I believe that an Indian can learn all that is in the books of the white man, so that he may be equal to them in the ways of the mind!"

I studied harder than most of the boys. Missionaries were poor, and the Government policy of education for the Indian had not then been developed. The white man in general had no use for the Indian. Sitting Bull and the Northern Cheyennes were still fighting in Wyoming and Montana, so that the outlook was not bright for me to pursue my studies among the whites; yet it was now my secret dream and ambition.

It was at Santee that I sawed my first cord of wood. Before long I had a little money of my own, for I sawed most of Dr. Riggs's own wood and some at the Dakota Home, besides other work for which I was paid. Although I could not understand or speak much English, at the end of my second year I could translate every word of my English studies into the native tongue, besides having read all that was then published in the Sioux. I had caught up with boys who had two or three years the start of me, and was now studying elementary algebra and geometry.

One day Dr. Riggs came to me and said that he had a way by which he could send me to Beloit, Wisconsin, to enter the preparatory department of Beloit College. This was a great opportunity, and I grasped it eagerly, though I had not yet lost my old timidity about venturing alone among the white people.

On the eve of departure, I received word from Flandreau that my father was dead, after only two days' illness. He was still in the prime of life and a tireless worker. This was a severe shock to me, but I felt even more strongly that I must carry out his wishes. It was clear that he who had sought me out among the wild tribes at the risk of his life, and set my feet in the new trail, should be obeyed to the end. I did not go back to my home, but in September, 1876, I started from Santee to Beloit to begin my serious studies.

FOR DISCUSSION

1. Tell what you think were some basic differences between the white man's world and the Sioux civilization. Use incidents or examples from the selection to support your answer.

2. Do you think Eastman could have fulfilled his wishes to "learn all that is in the books of the white man, so that he may be equal to them in the ways of the mind" and still retain his Indian values? Defend your answer.

Thomas S. Whitecloud

1914–1972

Born in New York City, Thomas St. Germain Whitecloud spent much of his youth on the Lac du Flambeau Chippewa Reservation in Wisconsin. After a troubled boyhood, during which he was expelled from several Indian schools, he finally decided upon medicine as a career. Struggling to raise his grades for admission to medical school, he first attended the University of New Mexico and ultimately was graduated from the University of Redlands in California. In 1939 he was accepted for admission to Tulane University Medical School, where he received his M.D.

Dr. Whitecloud worked for a time as a physician with the Indian Service and then established a private practice in Texas, where for more than seven years he was the only doctor in an entire county. After his retirement from general practice, Dr. Whitecloud served as a ship's surgeon, founded the Three Feathers Society, an Indian corresponding group, and was instrumental in the establishment of the American Association of Indian Physicians. At the time of his death, he was a consultant for the Commission on Alcoholism and Drug Abuse for Indians, under the Department of Health, Education and Welfare.

"Blue Winds Dancing," written while he was a college student, won first prize in a Phi Beta Kappa essay contest in 1938.

Blue Winds Dancing

There is a moon out tonight. Moon and stars and clouds tipped with moonlight. And there is a fall wind blowing in my heart. Ever since this evening, when against a fading sky I saw geese wedge southward. They were going home.... Now I try to study, but against the pages I see them again, driving southward. Going home.

Across the valley there are heavy mountains holding up the night sky, and beyond the mountains there is home. Home, and peace, and the beat of drums, and blue winds dancing over snow fields. The Indian lodge will fill with my people, and our gods will come and sit among them. I should be there then. I should be at home.

But home is beyond the mountains, and I am here. Here where fall hides in the valleys and winter never comes down from the mountains. Here where all the trees grow in rows; the palms stand stiffly by the roadsides, and in the groves the orange trees line in military rows and endlessly bear fruit. Beautiful, yes; there is always beauty in order, in rows of growing things! But it is the beauty of captivity. A pine fighting for existence on a windy knoll is much more beautiful.

In my Wisconsin, the leaves change before the snows come. In the air there is the smell of wild rice and venison cooking; and when the winds come whispering through the forests, they carry the smell of rotting leaves. In the evenings, the loon calls, lonely; and birds sing their last songs before leaving. Bears dig roots and eat late fall berries, fattening for their long winter sleep. Later, when the first snows fall, one awakens in the morning to find the world white and beautiful and clean. Then one can look back over his trail and see the tracks following. In the woods there are tracks of deer and snowshoe rabbits and long streaks where partridges slide to alight. Chipmunks make tiny footprints on the limbs; and one can hear squirrels busy in hollow trees, sorting acorns. Soft lake waves wash the shores, and sunsets burst each evening over the lakes and make them look as if they were afire.

That land which is my home! Beautiful, calm—where there is no hurry to get anywhere, no driving to keep up in a race that knows no ending and no goal. No classes where men talk and talk, and then stop now and then to hear their own words come back to them from the students. No constant peering into the maelstrom[1] of one's mind; no worries about grades and honors; no hysterical preparing for life until that life is half over; no anxiety about one's place in the thing they call Society.

I hear again the ring of axes in deep woods, the crunch of snow beneath my feet. I feel again the smooth velvet of ghost-birch bark. I hear the rhythm of the drums. . . . I am tired. I am weary of trying to keep up this bluff of being civilized. Being civilized means trying to do everything you don't want to, never doing anything you want to. It means dancing to the strings of custom and tradition; it means living in houses and never knowing or caring who is next door. These civilized white men want us to be like them—always dissatisfied, getting a hill and wanting a mountain.

Then again, maybe I am not tired. Maybe I'm licked. Maybe I am just not smart enough to grasp these things that go to make up civilization. Maybe I am just too lazy to think hard enough to keep up.

Still, I know my people have many things that civilization has taken from the whites. They know how to give, how to tear one's piece of meat in two and share it with one's brother. They know how to sing—how to make each man his own songs and sing them; for their music they do not have to listen to other men singing over a radio. They know how to make things with their hands, how to shape beads into design and make a thing of beauty from a piece of birch bark.

But we are inferior. It is terrible to have to feel inferior, to have to read reports of intelligence tests and learn that one's race is behind. It is terrible to sit in classes and hear men tell you that your people worship sticks of wood—that your gods are all false, that the Manitou[2] forgot your people and did not write them a book.

I am tired. I want to walk again among the ghost-birches. I want to see the leaves turn in autumn, the smoke rise from the lodge-houses, and to feel the blue winds. I want to hear the drums; I want to hear the drums and feel the blue whispering winds.

There is a train wailing into the night. The trains go across the mountains. It would be easy to catch a freight. They will say he

[1] maelstrom (māl' strəm): whirlpool.
[2] Manitou: Great Spirit.

has gone back to the blanket; I don't care. The dance at Christmas. . . .

A bunch of bums warming at a tiny fire talk politics and women and joke about the Relief and the WPA[3] and smoke cigarettes. These men in caps and overcoats and dirty overalls living on the outskirts of civilization are free, but they pay the price of being free in civilization. They are outcasts. I remember a sociology professor lecturing on adjustment to society; hobos and prostitutes and criminals are individuals who never adjusted, he said. He could learn a lot if he came and listened to a bunch of bums talk. He would learn that work and a woman and a place to hang his hat are all the ordinary man wants. These are all he wants, but other men are not content to let him want only these. He must be taught to want radios and automobiles and a new suit every spring. Progress would stop if he did not want these things. I listen to hear if there is any talk of communism or socialism in the hobo jungles. There is none. At best there is a sort of disgusted philosophy about life. They seem to think there should be a better distribution of wealth, or more work, or something. But they are not rabid about it. The radicals live in the cities.

I find a fellow headed for Albuquerque, and talk road-talk with him. "It is hard to ride fruit cars. Bums break in. Better to wait for a cattle car going back to the Middle West, and ride that." We catch the next east-bound and walk the tops until we find a cattle car. Inside, we crouch near the forward wall, huddle, and try to sleep. I feel peaceful and content at last. I am going home. The cattle car rocks. I sleep.

Morning and the desert. Noon and the Salton Sea, lying more lifeless than a mirage under a somber sun in a pale sky. Skeleton mountains rearing on the skyline, thrusting out of the desert floor, all rock and shadow and edges. Desert. Good country for an Indian reservation. . . .

Yuma and the muddy Colorado. Night again, and I wait shivering for the dawn.

Phoenix. Pima country. Mountains that look like cardboard sets on a forgotten stage. Tucson. Papago country. Giant cacti that look

[3] RELIEF . . . WPA: The WPA or Works Projects Administration was a Government agency organized in 1935 and designed to create jobs in order to relieve national unemployment.

like petrified hitchhikers along the highways. Apache country. At El Paso my road-buddy decides to go on to Houston. I leave him and head north to the mesa[4] country. Las Cruces and the terrible Organ Mountains, jagged peaks that instill fear and wondering. Albuquerque. Pueblos along the Rio Grande. On the boardwalk there are some Indian women in colored sashes selling bits of pottery. The stone age offering its art to the twentieth century. They hold up a piece and fix the tourists with black eyes until, embarrassed, he buys or turns away. I feel suddenly angry that my people should have to do such things for a living. . . .

Santa Fe trains are fast, and they keep them pretty clean of bums. I decide to hurry and ride passenger coal tenders. Hide in the dark, judge the speed of the train as it leaves, and then dash out, and catch it. I hug the cold steel wall of the tender and think of the roaring fire in the engine ahead and of the passengers back in the dining car reading their papers over hot coffee. Beneath me there is a blur of rails. Death would come quick if my hands should freeze and I fall. Up over the Sangre De Cristo range, around cliffs and through canyons to Denver. Bitter cold here, and I must watch out for Denver Bob. He is a railroad bull who has thrown bums from fast freights. I miss him. It is too cold, I suppose. On north to the Sioux country.

Small towns lit for the coming Christmas. On the streets of one I see a beam-shouldered young farmer gazing into a window filled with shining silver toasters. He is tall and wears a blue shirt, buttoned, with no tie. His young wife by his side looks at him hopefully. He wants decorations for his place to hang his hat to please his woman. . . .

Northward again. Minnesota, and great white fields of snow; frozen lakes and dawn running into dusk without noon. Long forests wearing white. Bitter cold, and one night the northern lights. I am nearing home.

I reach Woodruff at midnight. Suddenly I am afraid, now that I am but twenty miles from home. Afraid of what my father will say, afraid of being looked on as a stranger by my own people. I sit by a fire and think about myself and all other young Indians. We just don't seem to fit in anywhere—certainly not among the

---

[4] MESA (mā'sǝ): level-topped hill bounded wholly or in part by steep rock walls.

whites, and not among the older people. I think again about the learned sociology professor and his professing. So many things seem to be clear now that I am away from school and do not have to worry about some man's opinion of my ideas. It is easy to think while looking at dancing flames.

Morning. I spend the day cleaning up and buying some presents for my family with what is left of my money. Nothing much, but a gift is a gift, if a man buys it with his last quarter. I wait until evening, then start up the track toward home.

Christmas Eve comes in on a north wind. Snow clouds hang over the pines, and the night comes early. Walking along the railroad bed, I feel the calm peace of snowbound forests on either side of me. I take my time; I am back in a world where time does not mean so much now. I am alone; alone but not nearly so lonely as I was back on the campus at school. Those are never lonely who love the snow and the pines, never lonely when the pines are wearing white shawls and snow crunches coldly underfoot. In the woods I know there are the tracks of deer and rabbit; I know that if I leave the rails and go into the woods, I shall find them. I walk along feeling glad because my legs are light and my feet seem to know that they are home. A deer comes out of the woods just ahead of me and stands silhouetted on the rails. The North, I feel, has welcomed me home. I watch him and am glad that I do not wish for a gun. He goes into the woods quietly, leaving only the design of his tracks in the snow. I walk on. Now and then I pass a field, white under the night sky, with houses at the far end. Smoke comes from the chimneys of the houses, and I try to tell what sort of wood each is burning by the smoke; some burn pine, others aspen, others tamarack. There is one from which comes black coal smoke that rises lazily and drifts out over the tops of the trees. I like to watch houses and try to imagine what might be happening in them.

Just as a light snow begins to fall, I cross the reservation boundary; somehow it seems as though I have stepped into another world. Deep woods in a white-and-black winter night. A faint trail leading to the village.

The railroad on which I stand comes from a city sprawled by a lake—a city with a million people who walk around without seeing one another; a city sucking the life from all the country around; a city with stores and police and intellectuals and criminals and movies and apartment houses; a city with its politics and libraries and zoos.

Laughing, I go into the woods. As I cross a frozen lake, I begin to hear the drums. Soft in the night the drums beat. It is like the pulse beat of the world. The white line of the lake ends at a black forest, and above the trees the blue winds are dancing.

I come to the outlying houses of the village. Simple box houses, etched black in the night. From one or two windows soft lamplight falls on the snow. Christmas here, too, but it does not mean much; not much in the way of parties and presents. Joe Sky will get drunk. Alex Bodidash will buy his children red mittens and a new sled. Alex is a Carlisle man[5] and tries to keep his home up to white standards. White standards. Funny that my people should be ever falling farther behind. The more they try to imitate whites, the more tragic the result. Yet they want us to be imitation white men. About all we imitate well are their vices.

The village is not a sight to instill pride, yet I am not ashamed; one can never be ashamed of his own people when he knows they have dreams as beautiful as white snow on a tall pine.

Father and my brother and sister are seated around the table as I walk in. Father stares at me for a moment; then I am in his arms, crying on his shoulder. I give them the presents I have brought, and my throat tightens as I watch my sister save carefully bits of red string from the packages. I hide my feelings by wrestling with my brother when he strikes my shoulder in token of affection. Father looks at me, and I know he has many questions, but he seems to know why I have come. He tells me to go on alone to the lodge, and he will follow.

I walk along the trail to the lodge, watching the northern lights forming in the heavens. White waving ribbons that seem to pulsate with the rhythm of the drums. Clean snow creaks beneath my feet, and a soft wind sighs through the trees, singing to me. Everything seems to say, "Be happy! You are home now—you are free. You are among friends—we are your friends; we, the trees, and the snow, and the lights." I follow the trail to the lodge. My feet are

---

[5] CARLISLE MAN: graduate of the Carlisle School in Pennsylvania, the first reservation school, established by the Government in 1879.

light, my heart seems to sing to the music, and I hold my head high. Across white snow fields blue winds are dancing.

Before the lodge door I stop, afraid. I wonder if my people will remember me. I wonder— "Am I Indian, or am I white?" I stand before the door a long time. I hear the ice groan on the lake, and remember the story of the old woman who is under the ice, trying to get out, so she can punish some runaway lovers. I think to myself, "If I am white, I will not believe that story; if I am Indian, I will know that there is an old woman under the ice." I listen for a while, and I know that there is an old woman under the ice. I look again at the lights and go in.

Inside the lodge there are many Indians. Some sit on benches around the walls; others dance in the center of the floor around a drum. Nobody seems to notice me. It seems as though I were among a people I have never seen before. Heavy women with long black hair. Women with children on their knees—small children that watch with intent black eyes the movements of the dancers, whose small faces are solemn and serene. The faces of the old people are serene, too, and their eyes are merry and bright. I look at the old men. Straight, dressed in dark trousers and beaded velvet vests, wearing soft moccasins. Dark, lined faces intent on the music. I wonder if I am at all like them. They dance on, lifting their feet to the rhythm of the drums, swaying lightly, looking upward. I look at their eyes and am startled at the rapt attention to the rhythm of the music.

The dance stops. The men walk back to the walls and talk in low tones or with their hands. There is little conversation, yet everyone seems to be sharing some secret. A woman looks at a small boy wandering away, and he comes back to her.

Strange, I think, and then remember. These people are not sharing words—they are sharing a mood. Everyone is happy. I am so used to white people that it seems strange so many people could be together without someone talking. These Indians are happy because they are together, and because the night is beautiful outside, and the music is beautiful. I try hard to forget school and white people, and be one of these—my people. I try to forget everything but the night, and it is a part of me; that I am one with my people and we are all a part of something universal. I watch eyes and see now that the old people are speaking to me. They nod slightly, imperceptibly, and their eyes laugh into mine. I look around the room. All the eyes are friendly; they all laugh. No one questions my being here. The drums begin to beat again, and I catch the invitation in the eyes of the old men. My feet begin to lift to the rhythm, and I look out beyond the walls into the night and see the lights. I am happy. It is beautiful. I am home.

FOR DISCUSSION

1. The author says of himself and other young Indians, "We just don't seem to fit in anywhere. . . ." What aspects of the white man's society does he object to? How is he, at times, made to feel ashamed of his people?

2. What does going home signify for the author? Why does Whitecloud prefer the natural beauty of his homeland to the environment of his college campus?

Alonzo Lopez

b. 1947

A full-blooded Papago Indian, Alonzo Lopez was born in Crowhang Village, Arizona. He attended public school in Sells, Arizona, through the ninth grade and was then admitted to the Institute of American Indian Arts, in Santa Fe, New Mexico, from which he was graduated in 1967. From there Mr. Lopez went on to study at Yale and Wesleyan University in Connecticut.

Direction

I was directed by my grandfather
To the East,
   so I might have the power of the bear;
To the South,
   so I might have the courage of the eagle;
To the West,
   so I might have the wisdom of the owl;
To the North,
   so I might have the craftiness of the fox;
To the Earth,
   so I might receive her fruit;
To the Sky,
   so I might lead a life of innocence.

FOR DISCUSSION

Who do you think the "grandfather" in the poem is?

69

Emerson Blackhorse Mitchell and T. D. Allen

b. 1908   b. 1945

Emerson Blackhorse Mitchell, a Navaho Indian, was born near Shiprock, New Mexico, and was brought up by his grandparents. He spoke only the Navaho language until the age of six, attended public school, and in 1962 was admitted to the Institute of American Indian Arts in Santa Fe.

At the Institute he met Mrs. Terry Allen, the creative-writing instructor. She and her husband, Don Allen, had lived among, studied, and written about Indians for many years. She encouraged Emerson Mitchell to write the story of his boyhood; from this assignment emerged the book Miracle Hill: The Story of a Navaho Boy, *published in 1967.*

Mr. Mitchell attended Fort Lewis College in Durango, Colorado, and Navaho Community College in Many Farms, Arizona. He has been a community worker in Chinle, Arizona. Recently, as a social science instructor at a reservation school, he has been teaching Navaho culture—in the Navaho language. Mrs. Allen now directs the Creative Writing Project for the Bureau of Indian Affairs, and she also lectures at the University of California, Santa Cruz.

The following selection is from Miracle Hill.

I Do Have a Name

It was in the year of 1945 on a cold morning, the third day in the month of March. A little boy was born as the wind blew against the hogan[1] with bitter colds and the stars were disappearing into the heaven.

The little puff of smoke was gradually floating skyward. The floor of the earth was hard as ever with a few stripes of white snow still frozen to the gray-colored ground. With a queer squeaking, the baby awakes. His eyes were as dark as the colors of the ashes. His face is pink.

Following year, it was May and the bright sun shines in the land of enchantment close to the Four Corners, which was about thirty miles away. Four Corners is where the four states meets. They are New Mexico, Arizona, Utah, and Colorado.

The boy stood on his two little fat legs. Part of the time he crawl, but mostly he walks against chairs and his grandmother's loom. Very many lambs jumps and plays near the tent. The boy sometimes play with the lambs and goats. They smell like a wet dry dirt and the smell of corral.

But life was hard. Year after year the boy, his grandmother, and grandfather moved to various part of the reservation area. The boy was four now and begins to wonder, as he looks in the yonder valley and in the afar distance. With his sharp, dark brown eyes he would stand against the tree-shade house and look.

Day by day and step by step he learns different things. Very often grandfather would say, "My beloved child, when you grow big, I got a surprise for you, Little One."

The boy would smile and sits on his grandfather's lap.

But still, the boy would go to the hill and look into the distance, wondering when will he ever be there to see the place. The days were long, and as he herd his flock of sheeps, he began to think about things that were around him.

As the summer has gone by suddenly, they moved back to the mesa, where during winter it is warm and partly cold. The winter

[1] HOGAN: earth-covered Navaho dwelling, often round in shape.

slowly passes. When the boy herd sheep, he would play with the shepherd dogs and sometimes his pet lamb. Still yet he hasn't learn much, but he knew every tree and mountain passage through the great forest.

Very often when he herd sheep, he would play bareback on the branch of a springy cedar branch which would throw him off. When he feel like playing, he would make his own toys out of clay. They were yellow, gray, orange, and blue. These were the color of his toys which are made by his own five fingers.

Many times he hunted rabbit and animals, carrying his four-feet bow and arrow. It belonged to his grandfather, who had given it to him for a birthday present. First, he learned how to shoot the flying arrow. It was taught by his grandfather. He was very skill at shooting the arrow.

Since the boy is too small, he would sit and put his bow at the front of his feet and stretch the bowstring to shoot the arrow. Surely enough, the arrow flies like a diving eagle bound to catch a rabbit.

With his practice of shooting arrow, it gave him more and more ideas. While herding sheep he would shoot trees, imagining it as a huge lion, bear, and such. With his ability of learning, he quickly learn how to jump from rock to rock. He could run like an antelope when he runs into rocky hills and forest and down the rocky hillside.

When the boy was six years old, of what he has learn, he never forgets. But he has never seen yet much of a white man's ways. Then one day he came home, carry a loads of rabbit in his bag made of buckskin.

Grandmother stood outside the hogan. "How many rabbit did you kill?" she asked, grinning.

"Oh, I kill six."

Then in English she spoke. "Oh, six."

The boy dropped the bag and put down his arrow bag and bow against the hogan. "Grandmother! What's that word mean?"

"What word?" said grandmother.

"The word *ce-e-ex*," said the boy.

Then she laugh as though the whole mountainside crushing. She dance around a little bit and sang an old song, saying, "Oh, twinle, twinle, little star."

"Grandmother, are you going nuts or something?" the boy asked, "or is it you feeling happy because grandfather's coming home today?"

"No, Little One," she said.

Then the boy stand up against the hogan. He didn't know that his grandmother had been a student once. Now, grandmother never spoke none of a white man's tongue. "Grandmother," he said.

"Quiet, Little One. Go get some water from the spring. Then I'll answer your question," she said.

The boy pick up the bag and runs down the hill into the forest with a white water bag made of goatskin. With his skill, he has no problem of running swiftly and no problem of falling. It was a mile and a half.

At the spring he filled up his water bag and started walking up the hill. He saw his grandfather riding his horse through the canyon in the yonder hills.

The boy thought of an idea that he would have a race with him. So, with a quick jerk, he put the bag on the shoulder and jumps on the rock. Like he always did, he made the short cut, doing nothing but jumping from rock to rock. When he got home, grandmother was preparing a meal outside the hogan.

She turns around with her hands on her waist, holding a big silver spoon. "What did you do," she said, "fly or something?"

"No, I ran," he said.

"Impossible," she said.

The boy sits on the log of an old cedar, his pants all dirty and shirt sleeves torn off on both sides, and wearing a white headband with a black eagle feather. He laughs at his grandmother.

"What is it?" she said.

"Oh, nothing," he said, "it just that, I didn't know you can speak a white tongue! So now would you tell me what the word *six* mean?"

"It means six rabbit," she said. "Six mean six." She picks up a stick and writes figures in the sandy dust—1, 2, 3, 4, 5, 6—counting as she writes.

"One," the boy said, and, "six." Then, "What do you call this?"

"That's a bucket," she said. "Now enough of that."

"Ooh, my grandfather coming," the boy said.

"Where?"

"See, there he is down yonder."

She is stirring up the mutton soup, and on her left hand she holds a dough in a form of a ball. The soup smelled with vegetable, and the smell of fried bread made the boy grow hungrier than ever as she stack the brownish bread in a white plate. She was putting another stick and more in the fireplace to burn.

"Little One, get me the broom and I'll teach your grandfather a lesson that he'll never forgets," she said. "He never thinks of us. He's always going."

The boy went back into the hogan and closed the door. As he peep through an opening of the door, grandfather got knock off the horse, and grandmother quickly grabs the broom and hits grandfather again. Then she throws the rubbery dough into grandfather's face.

"Take that," she said.

The boy just laugh in the hogan, and suddenly grandmother said, "Time to eat."

While they were eating, grandfather said, "We're moving to summer home."

"Where we used to live in a tent?" the boy asked.

"No," grandfather said. "We are leaving tomorrow noon, and your uncle is coming on the pickup to haul our blankets, dishes, and few lambs that are small."

Yes, surely enough, it was the next morning. As grandmother and grandfather packed the bundle of blankets and suitcases, clothes, putting and setting boxes in place.

It was a good day for traveling.

"Little One, take the sheep out of the corral and get a head start," said grandfather.

As he opened the gate to let the sheep out, the boy look up the valley and down the steep canyon. He wondered as he stands there, wearing his white shirt, carry a big bow in his hand. The arrow were kind of heavy, but he was used to carrying it all the time. He kept saying the word *six*, and *one* and *bucket*, as he stroll after the sheeps down the grassland.

It looked like a green pasture with a stream of water. Only the prairie dogs barked in the far distance at the edge of the woods where there is an open sight. The boy didn't like prairie dogs. The crows flew across the blue sky as the white cloud are moving eastward like a big white sheep in the grazing land.

Down into the canyon he walks and jumps from rocks to rocks as he's going after the flock of sheep. He would ask himself, "What will I do when I'm seven years old next year?"

He wanted to speak English, but how would he learn? He would say, "When I was young, which was two years ago, I used to wondered about that rock down yonder. I have been there a few times now. Surely, there is a way," he said to himself.

Finally he brought his sheep to the edge of the mesa. It was around about three o'clock now. All this time he didn't know he has gone many miles with the sheep. The dust of clouds were up in the air like a dust storm. He didn't mind walking in it. Many times he rested.

Then finally it was getting dark as he arrive with his sheep at the next spring, which has a bitter taste. It's good only for sheep, so the poor boy has to thirst until grandmother and grandfather arrive. He waited and waited until late. He heard horse hoofs beating against the hard floor of the earth. The sheep rested quietly and the dogs barked. And the big yellow moon shined as the stars twinkle above.

The rumbling sound grew louder and louder. The owl hoot in the brushes. There were bushes and tall grass. Soon the boy saw them approach. It was grandmother and grandfather riding horses along the road. Then they turn off the road and headed towards the spring. As they watered their horses, they joined with the boy.

"We'll make it tonight," said grandfather, "but first, you must eat."

Grandmother built a fire and putted the sandwich aside for the boy to eat. There were roast mutton, baked potatoes, and biscuit. Now it was around nine o'clock.

As soon as they had eaten, they started off for another journey which will surely take until the morning. The sheep knew their pack so they were going single file along the road.

The boy fell asleep sitting behind his grandfather. Part of the time he would almost fall off; his head goes this way and that way. He didn't know that he was asleep until he wake up in a tent where he has never been before, or nor seen the place.

It was morning. Grandfather snores while grandmother was outside making coffee and tortillas.[2]

[2] TORTILLAS (tôr·tē'yäs): thin pancakes, served hot with various fillings.

The boy went out to see the place, to see what it is like. As for him, he'd never seen a water tower, or big building, and real green trees. As he runs to the top of the hill, he could now see distance away. For many years he had seen Shiprock stand, but had never looked what was below and beyond. It was for the first time he is seeing buildings and towns. There were smokes going up in the air. In about four miles there runs a river. He could heard many ducks and various kind of sounds by the river.

He rushes back to grandmother and asks, "What are the building and great tower like a ball in the air?"

Grandmother said, "They are town, and many people live there, and your mother lives there at the farm."

"My mother?" said the boy. "I don't know her."

Then grandmother calls to grandfather, "Get up and tell the Little One about his mother."

"Come, Little One, let's go up the hill and let me tell you more about the place," grandfather said.

The boy and grandfather first had a cup of coffee, as grandmother sweeps the hard earth floor outside under the shade house. Grandfather stretch himself and then gets hold of the boy's hand and went up the hill.

At the top, the boy again looks across the hills. Grandfather sat down with his leg crossed. The boy sit besides his grandfather like a pet dog.

"Your aunt is coming on horseback before noon," said grandfather, "and she's bringing watermelons and fresh green corns and a few vegetables."

At that moment, the boy sees his aunt riding in a distance. His grandfather said, "How do you know it's her?"

"Because I know it's her by the color of the horse." The horse was black and walks like he's about ready to take off on a racetrack. The boy turns and looks at his grandfather with his eyes twinkling. "Grandfather?" he said, "tell me about my mother."

"Oh, yes," grandfather said, smiling at him. "Sit down and let me tell you."

The boy sit against a brush.

"Your mother, Emma, has left you when you were eleven month old. She only went and took your brother with her."

"I had a brother?" said the boy. "I have a brother," he repeated it several times. "Then grandmother isn't my mother," he said, "and you aren't, aren't my father."

"Your father was killed," he said, "during World War II in oversea."

"My father was killed." The boy quiet down and looked at his grandfather.

Then grandfather looked up and said, "Your father was a very kind man. Before he left, he made many plans, but he was killed." He wipe his tears.

The boy got up and looked below the foot of the hill. There were four kids playing. "Grandfather, let's go back to the tent," he said, "and see my aunt."

Grandfather gets up and hold the boy's hand. Grandfather didn't feel too well.

When they reached the house, Aunt Amy greet her father. "Oh, father, I was late coming 'cause I was irrigating and plowing the field, and I had planted more corns," she said.

Grandmother was fixing a loom with yarn of colored strings to weave another rug.

The boy stood against a post which was there to hold up the shade house. He wondered why his grandfather didn't told him more about his mother, or where she is now. Nor he didn't know he had a cousin too, until his aunt told him that she had a daughter, and she has no father too.

The boy asked, "What has happen to her father?"

Aunt Amy said, "My husband was the brother of your father. He has gone four years ago, and never came back."

"What's her name?"

"Her name is Annie," Aunt Amy said. "And she's coming to see us tomorrow and live here with her grandmother too."

Later Amy was preparing meal as the sheep were in the green grassland over yonder on the tiny hills. By now it was getting hot, and the ground is getting hotter too. On the north side of the tent there were blooming flowers; colors were red and pink. Very often grandmother would go out and get the blooming flowers and chop them into tiny bites and cook it, and when it's cooled, she would serve it for dessert. It tasted sweet and part sour.

"Aunt Amy," the boy said.

"What is it?" she said.

"Why do they call me Little One?"

"I don't know. I suppose because you're small," she replied.

"Why don't I have a name?" asked the boy, as he look at his aunt making a vegetable soup. She didn't stop. She went ahead and continue about her work. And grandmother was busy rolling up more strings. She was ready to weave. Grandfather sleeps and snores.

"Do I have a name?" the boy said slowly, as he looked down at his moccasins.

"Yes," she said.

"I do have a name," he said, as he smile shyly.

Amy turned around and grinned. Then she said, "You were named after a colt that was born on the same day you were born. So your grandfather named you Broneco."

"Broneco," the boy said, and giggle with his hand over his mouth.

FOR DISCUSSION

1. Do you think the use of "Indian dialect" in the story is an effective literary device? Explain.

2. Why do the English words Broneco learns seem so important to him? Why do you think he has waited until this time to ask if he has a name?

Patty Harjo

b. 1947

Patty Harjo, whose Indian name is Ya-ka-nes, was born in Miami, Oklahoma, of Seminole and Seneca descent. She attended public school in Oklahoma and was admitted to the Institute of American Indian Arts in 1967. After graduating from the Institute, second in a class of sixty-one students, Miss Harjo entered a museum internship training program at the University of Colorado Museum in Boulder, Colorado.

Who Am I?

"Who am I?" This is a question I have asked myself many times.

I am my parents and their parents and all their ancestors before them. I am all the people I have ever met, and I am going to be all the people I will ever meet. Also, I am all the forces and objects with which I come in contact. I am the wind, the trees, the birds, and the darkness.

I was born of two heritages—both proud, both noble. They clung to their ancient cultures—one a wolf, one a snake—North and South. Their ancestral roots were transplanted to a new land of adjustment, grief, pain, and sorrow, to a future unknown.

Theirs was a future that seemed only a candle in the darkness, a candle of hope for a new beginning. This was a land of disappointment. It was unlike the old. This was a land called Indian

Territory and then Oklahoma. In this land all tribes became one, all cultures and heritages began moving onward toward the sun.

Now our sun shines bright; our future is growing clear. We hide our grief, pain, and fears. We are moving on. We try to grasp the good of our heritage. We try to grasp our culture that has slipped away.

We ask, "Who am I?" and our answer comes to us from the distance, "You are all the things you have ever known and will ever know."

FOR DISCUSSION

How has the author related her culture's history to her own life? What does she mean by the statement "Now our sun shines bright . . ."?

Juanita Platero and Siyowin Miller

A writer himself, Chief Standing Bear of the Lakota tribe introduced Juanita Platero, a Navaho, and Siyowin Miller in 1929. In
the years since then, the two women have combined their literary
talents to produce many fine short stories as well as the novel The
Winds Erase Your Footprints. Much of their writing depicts the
Navaho's struggle to live in harmony with the divergent cultures
of the Navaho and the white man. "Chee's Daughter" first appeared in the magazine Common Ground.

Chee's Daughter

The hat told the story, the big, black, drooping Stetson. It was
not at the proper angle, the proper rakish angle for so young a
Navaho. There was no song, and that was not in keeping either.
There should have been at least a humming, a faint, all-to-himself
"he he he heya," for it was a good horse he was riding, a slender-
legged, high-stepping buckskin that would race the wind with light
knee-urging. This was a day for singing, a warm winter day, when
the touch of the sun upon the back belied the snow high on distant
mountains.

Wind warmed by the sun touched his high-boned cheeks like
flicker feathers, and still he rode on silently, deeper into Little
Canyon, until the red rock walls rose straight upward from the
stream bed and only a narrow piece of blue sky hung above.

81

Abruptly the sky widened where the canyon walls were pushed back to make a wide place, as though in ancient times an angry stream had tried to go all ways at once.

This was home—this wide place in the canyon—levels of jagged rock and levels of rich red earth. This was home to Chee, the rider of the buckskin, as it had been to many generations before him.

He stopped his horse at the stream and sat looking across the narrow ribbon of water to the bare-branched peach trees. He was seeing them each springtime with their age-gnarled limbs transfigured beneath veils of blossom pink; he was seeing them in autumn laden with their yellow fruit, small and sweet. Then his eyes searched out the indistinct furrows of the fields beside the stream, where each year the corn and beans and squash drank thirstily of the overflow from summer rains. Chee was trying to outweigh today's bitter betrayal of hope by gathering to himself these reminders of the integrity of the land. Land did not cheat! His mind lingered deliberately on all the days spent here in the sun caring for the young plants, his songs to the earth and to the life springing from it—". . . In the middle of the wide field . . . Yellow Corn Boy . . . He has started both ways . . . ," then the harvest and repayment in full measure. Here was the old feeling of wholeness and of oneness with the sun and earth and growing things.

Chee urged the buckskin toward the family compound where, secure in a recess of overhanging rock, was his mother's dome-shaped hogan, red rock and red adobe like the ground on which it nestled. Not far from the hogan was the half-circle of brush like a dark shadow against the canyon wall—corral for sheep and goats. Farther from the hogan, in full circle, stood the horse corral made of heavy cedar branches sternly interlocked. Chee's long thin lips curved into a smile as he passed his daughter's tiny hogan squatted like a round Pueblo oven beside the corral. He remembered the summer day when together they sat back on their heels and plastered wet adobe all about the circling wall of rock and the woven dome of piñon[1] twigs. How his family laughed when the Little One herded the bewildered chickens into her tiny hogan as the first snow fell.

Then the smile faded from Chee's lips and his eyes darkened

[1] PIÑON (pĭn'yōn): type of pine tree yielding edible, nutlike seeds.

as he tied his horse to a corral post and turned to the strangely empty compound. "Someone has told them," he thought, "and they are inside weeping." He passed his mother's deserted loom on the south side of the hogan and pulled the rude wooden door toward him, bowing his head, hunching his shoulders to get inside.

His mother sat sideways by the center fire, her feet drawn up under her full skirts. Her hands were busy kneading dough in the chipped white basin. With her head down, her voice was muffled when she said, "The meal will soon be ready, son."

Chee passed his father sitting against the wall, hat over his eyes as though asleep. He passed his older sister, who sat turning mutton ribs on a crude wire grill over the coals, noticed tears dropping on her hands. "She cared more for my wife than I realized," he thought.

Then because something must be said sometime, he tossed the black Stetson upon a bulging sack of wool and said, "You have heard, then." He could not shut from his mind how confidently he had set the handsome new hat on his head that very morning, slanting the wide brim over one eye: he was going to see his wife, and today he would ask the doctors about bringing her home; last week she had looked so much better.

His sister nodded but did not speak. His mother sniffled and passed her velveteen sleeve beneath her nose. Chee sat down, leaning against the wall. "I suppose I was a fool for hoping all the time. I should have expected this. Few of our people get well from the coughing sickness. But *she* seemed to be getting better."

His mother was crying aloud now and blowing her nose noisily on her skirt. His father sat up, speaking gently to her.

Chee shifted his position and started a cigarette. His mind turned back to the Little One. At least she was too small to understand what had happened, the Little One who had been born three years before in the sanitarium where his wife was being treated for the coughing sickness, the Little One he had brought home to his mother's hogan to be nursed by his sister, whose baby was a few months older. As she grew fat-cheeked and sturdy-legged, she followed him about like a shadow; somehow her baby mind had grasped that of all those at the hogan who cared for her and played with her, he Chee—belonged most to her. She sat cross-legged at his elbow when he worked silver at the forge; she rode before him in the saddle when he drove the horses to water; often she lay wakeful on her sheep pelts until he stretched out for the night in the darkened hogan and she could snuggle warm against him.

Chee blew smoke slowly, and some of the sadness left his dark eyes as he said, "It is not as bad as it might be. It is not as though we are left with nothing."

Chee's sister arose, sobs catching in her throat, and rushed past him out the doorway. Chee sat upright, a terrible fear possessing him. For a moment his mouth could make no sound. Then: "The Little One! Mother, where is she?"

His mother turned her stricken face to him. "Your wife's people came after her this morning. They heard yesterday of their daughter's death through the trader at Red Sands."

Chee started to protest, but his mother shook her head slowly. "I didn't expect they would want the Little One either. But there is nothing you can do. She is a girl child and belongs to her mother's people; it is custom."

Frowning, Chee got to his feet, grinding his cigarette into the dirt floor. "Custom! When did my wife's parents begin thinking about custom? Why, the hogan where they live doesn't even face the East!" He started toward the door. "Perhaps I can overtake them. Perhaps they don't realize how much we want her here with us. I'll ask them to give my daughter back to me. Surely, they won't refuse."

His mother stopped him gently with her outstretched hand. "You couldn't overtake them now. They were in the trader's car. Eat and rest, and think more about this."

"Have you forgotten how things have always been between you and your wife's people?" his father said.

That night, Chee's thoughts were troubled—half-forgotten incidents became disturbingly vivid—but early the next morning he saddled the buckskin and set out for the settlement of Red Sands. Even though his father-in-law, Old Man Fat, might laugh, Chee knew that he must talk to him. There were some things to which Old Man Fat might listen.

Chee rode the first part of the fifteen miles to Red Sands expectantly. The sight of sandstone buttes[1] near Cottonwood Spring

---

[2] BUTTES (by$\overline{oo}$ts): flat-topped hills rising abruptly above the surrounding area.

reddening in the morning sun brought a song almost to his lips. He twirled his reins in salute to the small boy herding sheep toward many-colored Butterfly Mountain, watched with pleasure the feathers of smoke rising against tree-darkened western mesas from the hogans sheltered there. But as he approached the familiar settlement sprawled in mushroom growth along the highway, he began to feel as though a scene from a bad dream was becoming real.

Several cars were parked around the trading store, which was built like two log hogans side by side, with red gas pumps in front and a sign across the tar-paper roofs: *Red Sands Trading Post— Groceries   Gasoline   Cold Drinks   Sandwiches   Indian Curios.* Back of the trading post an unpainted frame house and outbuildings squatted on the drab, treeless land. Chee and the Little One's mother had lived there when they stayed with his wife's people. That was according to custom—living with one's wife's people—but Chee had never been convinced that it was custom alone which prompted Old Man Fat and his wife to insist that their daughter bring her husband to live at the trading post.

Beside the Post was a large hogan of logs, with brightly painted pseudo-Navaho designs on the roof—a hogan with smoke-smudged windows and a garish blue door which faced north to the highway. Old Man Fat had offered Chee a hogan like this one. The trader would build it if he and his wife would live there and Chee would work at his forge making silver jewelry where tourists could watch him. But Chee had asked instead for a piece of land for a cornfield and help in building a hogan far back from the highway and a corral for the sheep he had brought to this marriage.

A cold wind blowing down from the mountains began to whistle about Chee's ears. It flapped the gaudy Navaho rugs which were hung in one long bright line to attract tourists. It swayed the sign *Navaho Weaver at Work* beside the loom where Old Man Fat's wife sat hunched in her striped blanket, patting the colored thread of a design into place with a wooden comb. Tourists stood watching the weaver. More tourists stood in a knot before the hogan where the sign said: *See Inside a Real Navaho Home   25¢.*

Then the knot seemed to unravel as a few people returned to their cars; some had cameras; and there against the blue door Chee saw the Little One standing uncertainly. The wind was plucking at her new purple blouse and wide green skirt; it freed truant strands of soft dark hair from the meager queue[3] into which it had been tied with white yarn.

"Isn't she cunning!" one of the women tourists was saying as she turned away.

Chee's lips tightened as he began to look around for Old Man Fat. Finally he saw him passing among the tourists collecting coins.

Then the Little One saw Chee. The uncertainty left her face, and she darted through the crowd as her father swung down from his horse. Chee lifted her in his arms, hugging her tight. While he listened to her breathless chatter, he watched Old Man Fat bearing down on them, scowling.

As his father-in-law walked heavily across the graveled lot, Chee was reminded of a statement his mother sometimes made: "When you see a fat Navaho, you see one who hasn't worked for what he has."

Old Man Fat was fattest in the middle. There was indolence in his walk even though he seemed to hurry, indolence in his cheeks so plump they made his eyes squint, eyes now smoldering with anger.

Some of the tourists were getting into their cars and driving away. The old man said belligerently to Chee, "Why do you come here? To spoil our business? To drive people away?"

"I came to talk with you," Chee answered, trying to keep his voice steady as he faced the old man.

"We have nothing to talk about," Old Man Fat blustered and did not offer to touch Chee's extended hand.

"It's about the Little One." Chee settled his daughter more comfortably against his hip as he weighed carefully all the words he had planned to say. "We are going to miss her very much. It wouldn't be so bad if we knew that *part* of each year she could be with us. That might help you too. You and your wife are no longer young people and you have no young ones here to depend upon." Chee chose his next words remembering the thriftlessness of his wife's parents, and their greed. "Perhaps we could share the care of this little one. Things are good with us. So much snow this year will make lots of grass for the sheep. We have good land for corn and melons."

[3] QUEUE (kyo͞o): braid; pigtail.

Chee's words did not have the expected effect. Old Man Fat was enraged. "Farmers, all of you! Long-haired farmers! Do you think everyone must bend his back over the shorthandled hoe in order to have food to eat?" His tone changed as he began to brag a little. "We not only have all the things from cans at the trader's, but when the Pueblos come past here on their way to town, we buy their salty jerked mutton, young corn for roasting, dried sweet peaches."

Chee's dark eyes surveyed the land along the highway as the old man continued to brag about being "progressive." *He* no longer was tied to the land. He and his wife made money easily and could *buy* all the things they wanted. Chee realized too late that he had stumbled into the old argument between himself and his wife's parents. They had never understood his feeling about the land— that a man took care of his land and it in turn took care of him. Old Man Fat and his wife scoffed at him, called him a Pueblo farmer, all during that summer when he planted and weeded and harvested. Yet they ate the green corn in their mutton stews, and the chili paste from the fresh ripe chilis, and the tortillas from the cornmeal his wife ground. None of this working and sweating in the sun for Old Man Fat, who talked proudly of his easy way of living—collecting money from the trader who rented this strip of land beside the highway, collecting money from the tourists.

Yet Chee had once won that argument. His wife had shared his belief in the integrity of the earth, that jobs and people might fail one, but the earth never would. After that first year she had turned from her own people and gone with Chee to Little Canyon.

Old Man Fat was reaching for the Little One. "Don't be coming here with plans for my daughter's daughter," he warned. "If you try to make trouble, I'll take the case to the government man in town."

The impulse was strong in Chee to turn and ride off while he still had the Little One in his arms. But he knew his time of victory would be short. His own family would uphold the old custom of children, especially girl children, belonging to the mother's people. He would have to give his daughter up if the case were brought before the headman of Little Canyon, and certainly he would have no better chance before a strange white man in town.

He handed the bewildered Little One to her grandfather who stood watching every movement suspiciously. Chee asked, "If I brought you a few things for the Little One, would that be making trouble? Some velvet for a blouse, or some of the jerky she likes so well ... this summer's melon?"

Old Man Fat backed away from him. "Well," he hesitated, as some of the anger disappeared from his face and beads of greed shone in his eyes. "Well," he repeated. Then as the Little One began to squirm in his arms and cry, he said, "No! No! Stay away from here, you and all your family."

The sense of his failure deepened as Chee rode back to Little Canyon. But it was not until he sat with his family that evening in the hogan, while the familiar bustle of meal preparing went on about him, that he began to doubt the wisdom of the things he'd always believed. He smelled the coffee boiling and the oily fragrance of chili powder dusted into the bubbling pot of stew; he watched his mother turning round crusty fried bread in the small black skillet. All around him was plenty—a half of mutton hanging near the door, bright strings of chili drying, corn hanging by the braided husks, cloth bags of dried peaches. Yet in his heart was nothing.

He heard the familiar sounds of the sheep outside the hogan, the splash of water as his father filled the long drinking trough from the water barrel. When his father came in, Chee could not bring himself to tell a second time of the day's happenings. He watched his wiry, soft-spoken father while his mother told the story, saw his father's queue of graying hair quiver as he nodded his head with sympathetic exclamations.

Chee's doubting, acrid thoughts kept forming: Was it wisdom his father had passed on to him, or was his inheritance only the stubbornness of a long-haired Navaho resisting change? Take care of the land and it will take care of you. True, the land had always given him food, but now food was not enough. Perhaps if he had gone to school, he would have learned a different kind of wisdom, something to help him now. A schoolboy might even be able to speak convincingly to this government man whom Old Man Fat threatened to call, instead of sitting here like a clod of earth it-self—Pueblo farmer indeed. What had the land to give that would restore his daughter?

In the days that followed, Chee herded sheep. He got up in the half-light, drank the hot coffee his mother had ready, then started the flock moving. It was necessary to drive the sheep a long way from the hogan to find good winter forage. Sometimes Chee met friends or relatives who were on their way to town or to the road camp where they hoped to get work; then there was friendly banter and an exchange of news. But most of the days seemed endless; he could not walk far enough or fast enough from his memories of the Little One or from his bitter thoughts. Sometimes it seemed his daughter trudged beside him, so real he could almost hear her footsteps—the muffled pad-pad of little feet clad in deer-hide. In the glare of a snowbank he would see her vivid face, brown eyes sparkling. Mingling with the tinkle of sheep bells he heard her laughter.

When, weary of following the small sharp hoof marks that crossed and recrossed in the snow, he sat down in the shelter of a rock, it was only to be reminded that in his thoughts he had forsaken his brotherhood with the earth and sun and growing things. If he remembered times when he had flung himself against the earth to rest, to lie there in the sun until he could no longer feel where he left off and the earth began, it was to remember also that now he sat like an alien against the same earth; the belonging-together was gone. The earth was one thing and he was another.

It was during the days when he herded sheep that Chee decided he must leave Little Canyon. Perhaps he would take a job silversmithing for one of the traders in town. Perhaps, even though he spoke little English, he could get a job at the road camp with his cousins; he would ask them about it.

Springtime transformed the mesas. The peach trees in the canyon were shedding fragrance and pink blossoms on the gentled wind. The sheep no longer foraged for the yellow seeds of chamiso[4] but ranged near the hogan with the long-legged new lambs, eating tender young grass.

Chee was near the hogan on the day his cousins rode up with the message for which he waited. He had been watching with mixed emotions while his father and his sister's husband cleared the fields beside the stream.

"The boss at the camp says he needs an extra hand, but he wants to know if you'll be willing to go with the camp when they move

---

[4] CHAMISO (chə•mē´sō): shrub which forms dense thickets.

it to the other side of the town?" The tall cousin shifted his weight in the saddle.

The other cousin took up the explanation. "The work near here will last only until the new cutoff beyond Red Sands is finished. After that, the work will be too far away for you to get back here often."

That was what Chee had wanted—to get away from Little Canyon—yet he found himself not so interested in the job beyond town as in this new cutoff which was almost finished. He pulled a blade of grass, split it thoughtfully down the center, as he asked questions of his cousins. Finally he said: "I need to think more about this. If I decide on this job, I'll ride over."

Before his cousins were out of sight down the canyon, Chee was walking toward the fields, a bold plan shaping in his mind. As the plan began to flourish, wild and hardy as young tumbleweed, Chee added his own voice softly to the song his father was singing:". . . In the middle of the wide field . . . Yellow Corn Boy . . . I wish to put in."

Chee walked slowly around the field, the rich red earth yielding to his footsteps. His plan depended upon this land and upon the things he remembered most about his wife's people.

Through planting time Chee worked zealously and tirelessly. He spoke little of the large new field he was planting, because he felt so strongly that just now this was something between himself and the land. The first days he was ever stooping, piercing the ground with the pointed stick, placing the corn kernels there, walking around the field and through it, singing, ". . . His track leads into the ground . . . Yellow Corn Boy . . . his track leads into the ground." After that, each day Chee walked through his field watching for the tips of green to break through; first a few spikes in the center and then more and more, until the corn in all parts of the field was above ground. Surely, Chee thought, if he sang the proper songs, if he cared for this land faithfully, it would not forsake him now, even though through the lonely days of winter he had betrayed the goodness of the earth in his thoughts.

Through the summer Chee worked long days, the sun hot upon his back, pulling weeds from around young corn plants; he planted squash and pumpkin; he terraced a small piece of land near his mother's hogan and planted carrots and onions and the moisture-loving chili. He was increasingly restless. Finally he told his family what he hoped the harvest from this land would bring him. Then the whole family waited with him, watching the corn: the slender graceful plants that waved green arms and bent to embrace each other as young winds wandered through the field, the maturing plants flaunting their pollen-laden tassels in the sun, the tall and sturdy parent corn with new-formed ears and a froth of purple, red, and yellow corn-beards against the dusty emerald of broad leaves.

Summer was almost over when Chee slung the bulging packs across two pack ponies. His mother helped him tie the heavy rolled pack behind the saddle of the buckskin. Chee knotted the new yellow kerchief about his neck a little tighter, gave the broad black hat brim an extra tug, but these were only gestures of assurance and he knew it. The land had not failed him. That part was done. But this he was riding into? Who could tell?

When Chee arrived at Red Sands, it was as he had expected to find it—no cars on the highway. His cousins had told him that even the Pueblo farmers were using the new cutoff to town. The barren gravel around the Red Sands Trading Post was deserted. A sign banged against the dismantled gas pumps: *Closed until further notice.*

Old Man Fat came from the crude summer shelter built beside the log hogan from a few branches of scrub cedar and the sides of wooden crates. He seemed almost friendly when he saw Chee.

"Get down, my son," he said, eyeing the bulging packs. There was no bluster in his voice today, and his face sagged, looking somewhat saddened, perhaps because his cheeks were no longer quite full enough to push his eyes upward at the corners. "You are going on a journey?"

Chee shook his head. "Our fields gave us so much this year, I thought to sell or trade this to the trader. I didn't know he was no longer here."

Old Man Fat sighed, his voice dropping to an injured tone. "He says he and his wife are going to rest this winter; then after that he'll build a place up on the new highway."

Chee moved as though to be traveling on, then jerked his head toward the pack ponies. "Anything you need?"

"I'll ask my wife," Old Man Fat said as he led the way to the shelter. "Maybe she has a little money. Things have not been too good with us since the trader closed. Only a few tourists come

this way." He shrugged his shoulders. "And with the trader gone—
no credit."

Chee was not deceived by his father-in-law's unexpected con-
fidences. He recognized them as a hopeful bid for sympathy and,
if possible, something for nothing. Chee made no answer. He was
thinking that so far he had been right about his wife's parents:
their thriftlessness had left them with no resources to last until
Old Man Fat found another easy way of making a living.

Old Man Fat's wife was in the shelter working at her loom. She
turned rather wearily when her husband asked with noticeable
deference if she would give him money to buy supplies. Chee
surmised that the only income here was from his mother-in-law's
weaving.

She peered around the corner of the shelter at the laden ponies,
and then she looked at Chee. "What do you have there, my son?"

Chee smiled to himself as he turned to pull the pack from one
of the ponies, dragged it to the shelter where he untied the ropes.
Pumpkins and hardshelled squash tumbled out, and the ears of
corn—pale yellow husks fitting firmly over plump ripe kernels,
blue corn, red corn, yellow corn, many-colored corn, ears and ears
of it—tumbled into every corner of the shelter.

"Yooooh," Old Man Fat's wife exclaimed as she took some of
the ears in her hands. Then she glanced up at her son-in-law. "But
we have no money for all this. We have sold almost everything
we own—even the brass bed that stood in the hogan."

Old Man Fat's brass bed. Chee concealed his amusement as he
started back for another pack. That must have been a hard parting.
Then he stopped, for, coming from the cool darkness of the hogan
was the Little One, rubbing her eyes as though she had been asleep.
She stood for a moment in the doorway, and Chee saw that she
was dirty, barefoot, her hair uncombed, her little blouse shorn of
all its silver buttons. Then she ran toward Chee, her arms outstretched. Heedless of Old Man Fat and his wife, her father caught
her in his arms, her hair falling in a dark cloud across his face,
the sweetness of her laughter warm against his shoulder.

It was the haste within him to get this slow waiting game played
through to the finish that made Chee speak unwisely. It was the
desire to swing her before him in the saddle and ride fast to Little
Canyon that prompted his words. "The money doesn't matter. You
still have something. . . ."

Chee knew immediately that he had overspoken. The old woman looked from him to the corn spread before her. Unfriendliness began to harden in his father-in-law's face. All the old arguments between himself and his wife's people came pushing and crowding in between them now.

Old Man Fat began kicking the ears of corn back onto the canvas as he eyed Chee angrily. "And you rode all the way over here thinking that for a little food we would give up our daughter's daughter?"

Chee did not wait for the old man to reach for the Little One. He walked dazedly to the shelter, rubbing his cheek against her soft dark hair, and put her gently into her grandmother's lap. Then he turned back to the horses. He had failed. By his own haste he had failed. He swung into the saddle, his hand touching the roll behind it. Should he ride on into town?

Then he dismounted, scarcely glancing at Old Man Fat, who stood uncertainly at the corner of the shelter, listening to his wife. "Give me a hand with this other pack of corn, grandfather," Chee said, carefully keeping the small bit of hope from his voice.

Puzzled, but willing, Old Man Fat helped carry the other pack to the shelter, opening it to find more corn as well as carrots and round, pale yellow onions. Chee went back for the roll behind the buckskin's saddle and carried it to the entrance of the shelter, where he cut the ropes and gave the canvas a nudge with his toe. Tins of coffee rolled out, small plump cloth bags; jerked meat from several butcherings spilled from a flour sack; and bright red chilis splashed like flames against the dust.

"I will leave all this anyhow," Chee told them. "I would not want my daughter nor even you old people to go hungry."

Old Man Fat picked up a shiny tin of coffee, then put it down. With trembling hands he began to untie one of the cloth bags—dried sweet peaches.

The Little One had wriggled from her grandmother's lap, unheeded, and was on her knees, digging her hands into the jerked meat.

"There is almost enough food here to last all winter," Old Man Fat's wife sought the eyes of her husband.

Chee said, "I meant it to be enough. But that was when I thought you might send the Little One back with me." He looked down at his daughter noisily sucking jerky. Her mouth, both fists, were full of it. "I am sorry that you feel you cannot bear to part with her."

Old Man Fat's wife brushed a straggly wisp of gray hair from her forehead as she turned to look at the Little One. Old Man Fat was looking too. And it was not a thing to see. For in that moment the Little One ceased to be their daughter's daughter and became just another mouth to feed.

"And why not?" the old woman asked wearily.

Chee was settled in the saddle, the barefooted Little One before him. He urged the buckskin faster, and his daughter clutched his shirtfront. The purpling mesas flung back the echo: ". . . My corn embrace each other. In the middle of the wide field . . . Yellow Corn Boy embrace each other."

FOR DISCUSSION

1. Compare Chee's values about family and money to those of Old Man Fat.

2. Discuss Chee's relationship to the land. What did he mean when he said, "Land did not cheat!"? Why did he lose faith in the land? What news and what efforts on his part cause him to regain his faith?

3. How do you think "Chee's Daughter" and the Navaho chant on the opposite page are related?

Navaho Chant

I am the White Corn Boy.
I walk in sight of my home.
I walk in plain sight of my home.
I walk on the straight path which is towards my home.
I walk to the entrance of my home.
I arrive at the beautiful goods curtain which hangs at the
    doorway.
I arrive at the entrance of my home.
I am in the middle of my home.
I am at the back of my home.
I am on top of the pollen footprint.
I am on top of the pollen seed print.
I am like the Most High Power Whose Ways Are Beautiful.
Before me it is beautiful,
Behind me it is beautiful,
Under me it is beautiful,
Above me it is beautiful,
All around me it is beautiful.

Durango Mendoza

b. 1945

A man whose creative talents extend into many fields, Durango Mendoza is a writer, a photographer, and an artist. Born in Oklahoma, he is the son of a Creek Indian mother and a Mexican-American father. At the age of thirteen he went to live in Kansas City, Missouri, where he was graduated from high school. He attended the University of Missouri in Columbia, where he won several writing awards and prizes, one of which was for the following selection, "Summer Water and Shirley." After graduating with an A. B. in creative writing, Mr. Mendoza attended the School of the Art Institute of Chicago with the aid of a Ford Foundation scholarship.

Mr. Mendoza now works as a picture editor for a publishing agency. "Photography fulfills many aspects of both writing and painting for me, but I hope to eventually return to school to complete the requirements so that I may teach. . . . I feel that soon I may be able to bring together all of what I have learned about writing, art and photography, and book publishing to produce a volume of my own."

Summer Water and Shirley

It was in the summer that had burned every stalk of corn and every blade of grass and dried up the creek until it only flowed in trickles across the ford below the house where in the pools the boy could scoop up fish in a dishpan.

96

The boy lived with his mother and his sister Shirley and the three smaller children eleven miles from Weleetka, and near Lthwathlee Indian church, where it was Eighth Sunday meeting and everyone was there. The boy and his family stayed at the camp house of his dead father's people.

Shirley and her brother, who was two years older and twelve, had just escaped the deacon and were lying on the brown, sunscorched grass behind the last camp house. They were out of breath and giggled as they peeped above the slope and saw the figure of the deacon, Hardy Eagle, walking toward the church house.

"Boy, we sure out-fooled him, huh?" Shirley laughed lightly and jabbed her elbow in her brother's shaking side. "Whew!" She ran her slim hand over her eyes and squinted at the sky. They both lay back and watched the cloudless sky until the heat in their blood went down and their breath slowed to normal. They lay there on the hot grass until the sun became too much for them.

"Hey, let's go down to the branch and find a pool to wade in, okay?" She had rolled over suddenly and spoke directly into the boy's ear.

"I don't think we better. Mama said to stay around the church grounds."

"Aw, you're just afraid."

"No, it's just that—"

" 'Mama said to stay around the church grounds!' Fraidycat, I'll go by myself then." She sat up and looked at him. He didn't move and she sighed. Then she nudged him. "Hey." She nudged him again and assumed a stage whisper. "Looky there! See that old man coming out of the woods?"

The boy looked and saw the old man shuffling slowly through the high johnson grass[1] between the woods and the clearing for the church grounds. He was very old and still wore his hair in the old way.

"Who is he?" Shirley whispered. "Who is he?"

"I can't tell yet. The heat makes everything blurry." The boy was looking intently at the old man, who was moving slowly in the weltering heat through the swaying grass that moved with the sound of light tinsel in the dry wind.

"Let's go sneak through the grass and scare him," Shirley suggested. "I bet that'd make him even run." She moved her arms

[1] JOHNSON GRASS: coarse grass, cultivated as fodder for animals.

as if she were galloping and broke down into giggles. "Come on,"
she said, getting to one knee.

"Wait!" He pulled her back.

"What do you mean, 'wait'? He'll be out of the grass pretty
soon and we won't—" She broke off. "What's the matter? What're
you doing?"

The boy had started to crawl away on his hands and knees and
was motioning for her to follow. "Come on, Shirley," he whispered.
"That's old Ansul Middlecreek!"

"Who's *he*?"

"Don't you remember? Mama said he's the one that killed Has-
kell Day—with witchcraft. He's a *stiginnee!*"[2]

"A *stiginnee*? Aw, you don't believe that, do you? Mama says
you can tell them by the way they never have to go to the toilet,
and that's where he's been. Look down there." She pointed to the
little unpainted house that stood among the trees.

"I don't care *where* he's been! Come on, Shirley! Look ! Oh,
my gosh! He saw you pointing!"

"I'm coming," she said, and followed him quickly around the
corner of the camp house.

They sat on the porch. Almost everyone was in for the afternoon
service, and they felt alone. The wind was hot and it blew from
the southwest. It blew past them across the dry fields of yellow
weeds that spread before them, up to the low hills that wavered
in the heat and distance. They could smell the dry harshness of
the grass, and they felt the porch boards hot underneath them.
Shirley bent over and wiped her face with the skirt of her dress.

"Come on," she said. "Let's go down to the creek branch before
that deacon comes back." She pulled at his sleeve and they stood
up.

"Okay," he said, and they skirted the outer camp houses and
followed the dusty road to the bridge, stepping from tuft to tuft
of scorched grass.

Toward evening and suppertime they climbed out of the dry
bed of the branch, over the huge boulders to the road, and started
for the camp grounds. The sun was in their eyes as they trudged
up the steep road from the bridge. They had found no water in

[2] *stiginnee*: practitioner of witchcraft, usually an old person who is reputedly able
to change forms and to act upon the minds of his victims.

the branch, so they had gone on down to the creek. For the most part it too was dry.

Suddenly they saw a shadow move into the dust before them. They looked up and saw old Ansul Middlecreek shuffling toward them. His cracked shoes raised little clouds of dust that rose around his ankles and made whispering sounds as he moved along.

"Don't look when you go by," the boy whispered intently, and he pushed her behind him. But as they passed by, Shirley looked up.

"Hey, Ansul Middlecreek," she said cheerfully. "*Henkschay!*"[3] Then with a swish of her skirt she grabbed her brother and they ran. The old man stopped, and the puffs of dust around his feet moved ahead as he grumbled, his face still in shadow because he did not turn around. The two didn't stop until they had reached the first gate. Then they slowed down, and the boy scolded his sister all the way to their camp. And all through supper he looked at the dark opening of the door and then at Shirley who sat beside him, helping herself with childish appetite to the heavy, greasy food that was set before her.

"You better eat some," she told her brother. "Next meetin's not 'til next month."

Soon after they had left the table, she began to complain that her head hurt, and their mother got them ready to go home. They took the two little girls and the baby boy from where they were playing under the arbor and cleaned them up before they started out. Their uncle, George Hulegy, would go with them and carry the biggest girl. The mother carried the other one, while the boy struggled in the rear with the baby. Shirley followed morosely behind them all as they started down the road that lay white and pale under the rising moon.

She began to fall further behind and shuffled her bare feet into the warm underlayer of dust. The boy gave to his uncle the sleeping child he carried and took Shirley by the hand, surprised that it was so hot and limp.

"Come on, Shirley, come on. Mama, Shirley's got a fever. Don't walk so fast—we can't keep up. Come on, Shirley," he coaxed. "Hurry."

They turned into their lane and followed it until they were on

---

[3] *Henkschay:* greeting such as "how are you," usually spoken heartily.

the little hill above the last stretch of road and started down its rocky slope to the sandy road below. Ahead, the house sat wanly under the stars, and Rey, the dog, came out to greet them, sniffing and wriggling his black body and tail.

George Hulegy and the mother were already on the porch as the boy led his sister into the yard. As they reached the porch, they saw the lamp begin to glow orange in the window. Then Shirley took hold of the boy's arm and pointed weakly toward the back yard and the form of the storehouse.

"Look, Sonny! Over there, by the storehouse." The boy froze with fear, but he saw nothing. "They were three little men," she said vaguely, and then she collapsed.

"Mama!" But as he screamed, he saw a great yellow dog with large brown spots jump off the other end of the porch with a click of its heavy nails and disappear into the shadows that led to the creek. The boy could hear the brush rustle and a few pebbles scatter as it went. Rey only whined uneasily and did not even look to where the creature had gone.

"What is it? What's wrong?" The two older persons had come quickly onto the porch, and the mother bent immediately to help her daughter.

"Oh, Shirley! George! Help me. Oh, gosh! She's burning up. Sonny, put back the covers of the big bed. Quick now!"

They were inside now and the boy spoke.

"She saw dwarfs," he said solemnly, and the mother looked at George Hulegy. "And there was a big yellow dog that Rey didn't even see."

"Oh, no, no," the mother wailed and leaned over Shirley, who had begun to writhe and moan. "Hush, baby, hush. Mama's here. Hush, baby; your mama's here." She began to sing softly a very old song while George Hulegy took a lantern from behind the stove.

"I'm going to the creek and get some pebbles where the water still runs," he said. "I have to hurry." He closed the screen quietly behind him, and the boy watched him as he disappeared with the swinging lantern, through the brush and trees, down into the darkness to the ford. Behind him the mother still sang softly as Shirley's voice began to rise, high and thin like a very small child's. The boy shivered in the heat and sat down in the corner to wait helplessly as he tried not to look at the dark space of the window.

He grew stiff and tired trying to control his trembling muscles as they began to jump.

Then George Hulegy came in with some pebbles that still were dripping, and they left little wet spots of dark on the floor as he placed them above all the doors and windows throughout the house. Finally he placed three round ones at the foot of the bed where Shirley lay twisting and crying with pain and fever.

The mother had managed to start a small fire in the kitchen stove and told the boy to go out and bring in a few pieces of cook wood from the woodpile. He looked at her and couldn't move. He stood stiff and alert and heard George Hulegy, who was bending close over Shirley, muttering some words that he could not understand. He looked at the door, but the sagging screen only reflected the yellow lamplight so that he couldn't see through into the darkness; he froze even tighter.

"Hurry, son!"

He looked at Shirley lying on the bed and moving from side to side.

"Sonny, I have to make Shirley some medicine!" His body shook from a spasm. The mother saw and turned to the door. "I'll get them," she said.

"Mama!"

She stopped and he barged through the door and found the darkness envelop him. As he fixed his wide-open gaze on the woodpile that faintly reflected the starlight and that of the moon which had risen above the trees, he couldn't look to either side, nor could he run. When he reached for the first piece of wood, the hysteria that was building inside him hardened into an aching bitter core. He squeezed the rough cool wood to his chest and felt the fibers press into his bare arms as he staggered toward the house and the two rectangles of light. The closer he came, the higher the tension inside him stretched, until he could scarcely breathe. Then he was inside again and he sat limply in the corner, light and drained of any support. He could feel nothing except that Shirley was lying in the big feather bed across the room, wailing with hurt and a scalding fever.

His mother was hurrying from the kitchen with a tin cup of grass tea when Shirley began to scream, louder and louder until the boy thought that he would never hear another sound, as he stood straight and hard, not leaning at all.

She stopped.

In the silence he saw his mother standing above and behind the lamp, casting a shadow on the ceiling, stopped with fear as they heard the other sound. The little girls had come into the room from their bedroom and were standing whimpering in their nightgowns by the door. The mother signaled and they became still and quiet, their mouths slightly open and their eyes wide. They heard nothing.

Then like a great, beating heart the sound rose steadily until they could smell the heat of a monstrous flesh, raw and hot. Steadily it grew to a gagging, stifling crescendo—then stopped. They heard the click of dog's nails on the porch's wooden planks, and afterwards, nothing. In the complete silence the air became cold for an instant, and Shirley was quiet.

It was three days now since Shirley had begun to die, and everyone knew how and had given up any hope. Even the white doctor could find nothing wrong, and all the old Indians nodded their solemn heads when he went away saying that Shirley would be up in a few days; for now, to them, her manner of death was confirmed. He said to send for him if there was any "real" change. No need to move her—there was nothing wrong—nothing physically wrong, he had said. He could not even feel her raging fever. To him, Shirley was only sleeping.

Everyone had accepted that Shirley was going to die, and they were all afraid to go near her. "There is evil around her," they said. They even convinced the mother to put her in the back room and close off all light and only open it after three days. She would not die until the third day's night, nor would she live to see the fourth day's dawn. This they could know. A very old woman spoke these words to the mother, and she could not disbelieve.

On this third day the boy sat and watched the flies as they crawled over the dirty floor, over the specks and splotches, the dust and crumbs. They buzzed and droned about some drops of water, rubbing their legs against themselves, nibbling, strutting, until the drops dried into meaningless little rings, while the hot wind blew softly through the open window, stirring particles of dust from the torn screen. A droplet of sweat broke away from above his eyebrow and ran a crooked rivulet down his temple until

he wiped it away. In his emptiness the boy did not want his sister
to die.

"Mama?"

"What is it, son?"

"Is Shirley going to die?"

"Yes, son."

He watched her as she stood with her back to him. She moved
the heavy skillet away from the direct heat and turned the damper
so that the flames would begin to die. She moved automatically,
as if faster movement would cause her to breathe in too much
of the stifling heat. And as she moved, the floor groaned under the
shift in weight, and her feet made whispering sounds against the
sagging boards. The flies still flitted about, mindless and nasty, as
the boy looked away from them to his mother.

"Does she have to, mama?"

"Shirley is dying, son."

Again he saw how the flies went about, unaware of the heat,
himself, his mother across the room, or that Shirley lay in her
silence in the back room. He splashed some more water from his
glass, and they knew he was there but immediately forgot and
settled back to their patternless walking about. And even though
the table was clean, they walked jerkily among the dishes and
inspected his tableware. The boy had lived all his life among these
creatures, but now he could not stand their nature.

"Darn flies!"

"Well, we won't have to worry when cold weather gets here,"
she said. "Now go call the kids and eat. I want to get some sewing
done this afternoon."

He said nothing and watched her as she went into the other
room. He went to the door and leaned out to call the small children. Then he slipped quietly into the back room and closed the
door behind him, fastening the latch in the dark. The heat was
almost choking, and he blinked away the saltiness that stung his
eyes. He stood by the door until he could see a little better. High
above his head a crack in the shingles filtered down a star of
daylight, and he stepped to the bed that stood low against the
rough planks of the wall. There were no flies in this room and
there was no sound.

The boy sat down on a crate and watched the face of his sister emerge from the gloom where she lay. Straining his eyes he finally saw the rough army blanket rise and fall, but so slight was the movement that when his eyes lost their focus, he could not see it, and he quickly put out his hand, but stopped. Air caught in his throat, and he stifled a cough, still letting his hand hover over the motionless face. Then he touched the smooth forehead and jerked his hand away as if he had been burned.

He sat and watched his sister's well-formed profile and saw how the skin of the nose and forehead had become taut and dry and now gleamed pale and smooth like old ivory in the semi-darkness. A smell like that of hot wood filled the room, but underneath it the boy could smell the odor of something raw, something evil— something that was making Shirley die.

The boy sat on the empty crate in the darkness through the late afternoon and did not answer when his mother called him. He knew that she would not even try the door to this room. He waited patiently for his thoughts to come together, not moving in the lifeless heat, and let the sweat flow from his body. He smelled the raw smell, and when it became too strong, he touched the smooth, round pebbles that had come from the creek where it still flowed, and the smell receded.

For many hours he sat, and then he got up and took down the heavy blanket that had covered the single window and let the moonlight fall across the face of his sister through the opening. He began to force his thoughts to remember, to relive every living moment of his life and every part that Shirley had lived in it with him. And then he spoke softly, saying what they had done, and how they would do again what they had done, because he had not given up, for he was alive, and she was alive, and they had lived and would *still* live. And so he prayed to his will and forced his will out through his thoughts and spoke softly his words and was not afraid to look out through the window into the darkness through which came the coolness of the summer night. He smelled its scents and let them touch his flesh and come to rest around the "only sleeping" face of his sister. He stood, watching, listening, living.

Then they came, silently, dark-bellied clouds drifting up from the south, and the wind, increasing, swept in the heavy scent of the approaching storm. Lightning flashed over the low, distant hills, and the clouds closed quietly around the moon as the thunder rumbled and the heavy drops began to fall, slowly at first, then irregularly, then increasing to a rhythmic rush of noise as the gusts of wind forced the rain in vertical waves across the shingled roof.

Much later, when the rain had moved ahead and the room became chilly, when the water began to drip from the roof and the countless leaves, the boy slipped out of his worn denim pants and took off his shirt and lay down beside his sister. She felt him and woke up.

"You just now gettin' to bed?" she asked. "It's pretty late for that, ain't it?"

"No, Shirley," he said. "Go on back to sleep. It'll be morning pretty soon, and when it gets light again, we'll go see how high the water's risen in the creek."

He pulled the cover over him and drew his bare arms beneath the blanket and pulled it over their shoulders as he turned onto his side. Lying thus he could see in the darkness the even darker shapes of the trees and the storehouse his father had built.

FOR DISCUSSION

1. Do you think it is possible that people like the *stiginnee* still exist? Were there forces of goodness in the story too? What were they? How would you account for Shirley's recovery at the end of the story?

2. What was the significance of water in the story?

Grey
Cohoe

b. 1944

Grey Cohoe is a Navaho Indian born in Tocito, New Mexico. After high school, he attended the Institute of American Indian Arts, where he distinguished himself in the fields of creative writing, painting, drawing, and printmaking. Although he has won numerous awards and prizes for his prose and poetry, his artistic talents have focused on printmaking. He has won top awards in the Scottsdale National Indian Arts Exhibition, and his prints have been exhibited both at the Arizona State Museum in Tucson and at the Smithsonian Institution in Washington, D. C. Mr. Cohoe was graduated from the University of Arizona in 1971.

"The Promised Visit" was written while he was a student at the Institute of American Indian Arts.

The Promised Visit

It had been a long day at Window Rock, Arizona. I'd shoved myself up at dawn and started from Shiprock early that morning. Today was a special day for me to appear for my tribal scholarship interview. I had applied for it in the spring so I could go on to school after my graduation from high school. My brother-in-law, Martin, was considerate enough to lend me his pickup truck. I would still have been there promptly for my appointment, no matter if I'd needed to walk, hitchhike, or crawl the hundred and twenty miles.

After all the waiting, I finally learned that I didn't need their scholarship to attend the school of my choice. I didn't need anything from them. They knew this all the time and didn't write to inform me. I was so sore about the unnecessary trip that I didn't bother to eat my lunch or supper. All I got was waste of time, money, and strength which I would've put to good use on the farm. Well, at least they wouldn't bother me, complaining about their money.

Gradually the warmth at the side of my face cooled off as the sunlight was broken up by long shadows across the plain, then bled over the fuzzy mountainous horizon. The same as yesterday—the usual sunny sky, the same quiet atmosphere, and the daily herding toils handled by the desert people—the daylight disappeared, ending another beautiful day. I didn't bother to glance a moment at the departing sun to give farewell or offer my traditional prayer for the kind sun, thanking him for his warmth and life. I constantly stared over the blue hood of the pickup onto the highway up ahead.

The old zigzagging road lined the shadowed flat region, cooling from a day's heat. It was not until now that the evening wind began to form the woollike clouds, building a dark overcast stretching across my destination. At first, it was obviously summer rain clouds, and even a child could recognize the rolling grayish mass. The white lane markers rhythmically speared under me as I raced toward home.

I rolled down the window about an inch to smell the first rain that I would inhale this summer. The harsh air rushed in, cold and wild. Its crazy current tangled and teased my hair. The aroma of the flying wet dirt tensed my warm nose, a smell of rain. Immediately the chill awakened my reflexes. I balanced my body into a proper driving position according to a statement in the driver's manual. I prepared to confront the slippery pavement.

[Because of] the long hard day, sitting and wrestling the stiff steering wheel, I was beaten. My muscles were too weak to fight the powerful wind, if a big thunderstorm should come upon me. I lazily moved one of my bare arms to roll up the window. I didn't like the roaring of the air leak. The chill of it made me tremble. I felt no fear of a gentle summer rain, but the dangerous hazards under a vigorous downpour frightened me.

I narrowed my eyes into the mirror to look back along the highway, hoping that someone else would be traveling along, too.

Unfortunately, no one showed up. I'd have to go all alone on this road with the next nearest gas station about ninety-eight miles. It was unusual, during such a vacationing summer, to find not a single tourist going on this route. Maybe, I thought, if I wait a few minutes, someone will show up; then I'll follow.

I lazily lifted my foot off the gas peddle and slowly stepped on the brakes. When I came to a stop, I gave a long stretch to relieve my stiffness. Then I yawned. I waited in hopes until the cool evening darkness filled the valley. I stood by the open car door and thought of how mysterious the storm looked. The more I waited, the more time I was wasting. Before long, after giving up waiting, I was on the road again. I sang some Navaho songs, whispered, and fitted my sweater around my shoulder. I did anything to accompany myself.

By now I could sight the lightnings spearing into the horizon, glowing against the dark overcast. I could almost see the whole valley in one flash. The black clouds came closer and angrier as I approached their overcast. Being used to the old reservation road, narrow and rough, and well adjusted to the pickup, I drove ahead to meet the first raindrops.

I thought of a joke and wanted to burst out in laughter, but only a smile came. I used to laugh when I teased my folks about my death. They would scold me and would arouse my superstitions about it. Speaking of your death is taboo. Now, when I wondered whether I'd ever make it to the other side of the storm, it didn't sound funny.

Many people had died along this same highway, never telling us what caused their accidents. Most of these tragedies occurred in bad weather, especially in thunderstorms. Several months ago the highway department stuck small white crosses along the road at each place where an accident victim was killed. This was to keep a driver alert and aware. The crosses became so numerous that it caused more confusion and more accidents. When a person sees a cross, he becomes nervous.

Every time we drove through the cross-lined highway, I would think of a parade. The invisible spectators sitting on their crosses would watch us go along. Many people believe that these ghosts bring bad luck. Of course, we Navahos get cursed by such witchcraft.

The dark clouds formed themselves into a huge ugly mass. It

reminded me of the myths the people feared in such angry clouds. The suspicious appearance scared me, making my joints and very soul tremble.

My stomach began to tighten up with a groaning sound. It made me weak. I imagined my sister's cooking at home. We'd butchered a sheep yesterday for meat supply. My sister had probably barbecued some mutton and made some fried bread. I swallowed down my empty throat and moved my empty stomach. The smell and taste of my imagined food seemed to be present in my mouth and nose. Restlessly, I speeded up a little faster.

The dark overcast hid my view of the road, and the area around faded away into darkness, so I had to turn on the headlights. My face was now tired of being fixed in the same direction, down the long, dirty highway. My eyelids were so weak that they closed by themselves. I should have slept longer last night. Again, I rolled down the window. The cold air poured in, caressing me with its moistened chill. It awoke me completely.

I would have brought my brother, Teddy, along to accompany me, but he was fast asleep so I didn't bother. I reckoned he'd rather work in the field than to sit all day long. Somehow, I was glad he hadn't come because I wouldn't want him to fear this killer storm. If anything should happen, I'd be the only one to die. Sadly, I kept on counting the dips, rocky hills, and the zigzagging curves as I drove on.

The sudden forceful blow jolted the car and waved it like a rolling wagon. The screaming wind began to knock at my windows. I clung hard on the steering wheel to fight the rushing wind. I slowed almost to a stop and peered out through the blowing dust at the hood, trying to keep on the road. Flying soil and tumbleweeds crashed against the car. I could not tell what ran beside the highway—a canyon or maybe a wash. The angry wind roared and blew so strong that the car slanted. I didn't know how to escape the Wind Monster. I sat motionless, feeling death inside my soul.

And then the car was rocked by falling raindrops as if it were a tin can being battered by flying stones. The downpour came too quickly for me to see the first drops on the windshield. The whole rocky land shook when a loud cracking lightning shot into the nearby ground.

"Oh, no! The devil is coming." I frightened myself, but I had

enough courage to pick up my speed a little, thinking that I might
escape his aim. I strained my eyes to see through the glare on the
windshield. The pouring raindrops were too heavy for the wipers.
It was like trying to look under water. Another swift stripe of
lightning exploded into the ground. This time, it was closer. I
kept myself from panicking. I drove faster, hoping the devil
wouldn't see me.

The storm calmed and turned into a genial shower. Then I could
see where I was. In sight, through the crystal rain, a green-and-
white lettered sign showed up in the headlights. LITTLEWATER
12 miles; SHIPROCK 32 miles. At last, I felt relieved. I would
be home in less than an hour. Never in my life did I ever long
for home so much until this day. The windshield cleared and the
rain had passed.

Again it was quiet, except this time I heard a splashing sound
at the tires. My ears missed the hard rhythms of smashing rain.
I felt as if I had been closely missed by a rifle shot.

Even though I didn't see any one of the monsters, still I looked
out, but shamefully, for the two rainbows. They weren't there. I
scolded myself for looking. It was ridiculous to fear something that
didn't exist, like fairies. Yes, I'd heard thunders, seen lightnings,
and felt the terrifying wind, but I'd come out alive. Only for a
moment was I trapped and my minutes numbered. I'd probably
confronted the stormhead.

"Standing ghost," I scoffed, and laughed to myself.

"It's too bad I can't see anything except the light-struck black
pavement," I thought. I always rejoiced to see and smell the land
where the rain had spread its tasteful water. It's refreshing to watch
the plants drink from the puddles around them.

I hoped the rain had traveled across the farmlands near Shiprock. I was supposed to irrigate the corn tomorrow, but luckily
the rain would take good care of it. I might do something else
instead. Maybe I'd go to the store or to the café and eat three
or four hamburgers. I liked to see that cute waitress there.

With the scary storm passing, and my being penetrated by the
superstition over, I felt as if I'd awakened from a nightmare. My
hunger, too, had surrendered, but the crampy stiffness still tightened my body. I didn't bother to stop for a rest. I rushed straight
home. I hoped my supper would be waiting. The clouds slid away
and it wasn't as late as I'd thought.

By now, some twinkling stars appeared over the northern horizon. The found moon cast its light on the soggy ground as the silky white clouds slid after the rain. The water reflected the light so that the standing water shone like the moon itself. I could see the whole area as if in daylight. I ran the tires through the shallow puddles on the pavement to feel it splash. I imagined myself running and playing along the San Juan river shore. I constantly hastened on, looking for the lights at Littlewater over on the other side of the next hill.

Littlewater is a small store standing alongside the highway. Besides the two trailer houses in the back of the store, there are several hogans and log cabins standing in view of the flat valley, but tonight I can see them only as dark objects at a distance. During warm wintry days, the local people gather together on the sunny side of the trading post walls to chat or watch the travelers stop for gas or supplies. But at this time in the summer, they all move to the cool mountains.

A few electric lights appeared within range of my headlights. Three dull guide lights shone at the store. One larger light showed up the whole front porch. As usual, there wasn't anybody around at this late hour of the night. I slowed to glance at the porch as I passed by. At the same time as I turned back to the road, I saw a standing object about fifty yards ahead. I had always feared dark objects at night. My soul tensed with frightening chill as I trembled. I drove closer, telling myself it would be a horse or a calf.

The lights reached the dark image as I approached. Surprisingly, it was a hitchhiker. I didn't think anything about the person. All that came to my mind was to offer someone my help. Then I saw it was a girl.

I stopped a little way past her.

She slowly and shyly walked to the car window. She was all wet and trembling from the cold air. "Can you give me a lift to Shiprock?" she politely asked in her soft, quivering voice.

"Sure. That's where I'm going too." I quickly offered the warm empty seat.

She smiled and opened the door. Water dripped to the floor from her wet clothes. She sat motionless and kept looking away from me.

I thought she was just scared or shy. I, too, was shy to look, and we didn't talk for a long time. It wasn't until a few miles from

Shiprock that I finally started a conversation.

"I guess the people around this area are happy to get such a big rain," I finally dared to utter. "I was supposed to water our farm field tomorrow, but I guess the good Lord did it for me," I joked, hoping she would laugh or say something. "What part of Shiprock are you from?" I questioned her.

"Not in Shiprock. About one mile from there," she carefully murmured, using the best of her English.

She looked uneducated by the style of the clothes she wore. She was dressed in a newly made green velvet blouse and a long, silky white skirt. She wore many silver and turquoise necklaces and rings. A red and orange sash-belt tightly fitted around her narrow waist. She was so dressed up that she looked ready for going to town or a squaw dance.

Her long black hair hung loosely to her small, round shoulder and beside her light-complexioned face. In the glow from the instrument panel I could tell she was very pretty. She didn't look like some other Navaho girls. Her skin was much lighter than their tannish-brown skin color.

Finally I gathered enough guts to offer her my school sweater. "Here. You better put this on before you catch cold. I hear pneumonia is very dangerous," I said, as I struggled about to take off the sweater.

She kindly took it and threw it around herself. "Thank you." She smiled and her words came out warmly.

I looked at her and she looked at the same time, too. I almost went off the road when I saw her beautiful smile of greeting. She was the prettiest girl I have ever seen. I jerked the steering wheel, and the car jolted back onto the highway. We both laughed. From that moment on, we talked and felt as if we'd known each other before. I fell in love and I guess she did, too.

"Where have you been in this kind of bad weather?" I began to ask questions so we could get better acquainted with each other.

"I visited some of my old relatives around Littlewater." She calmly broke her shyness. "The ground was too wet to walk on, so I decided to get a ride."

"I've been to Window Rock to get a scholarship to an art school. I started this morning and it isn't until now I'm coming back. I'm late for my supper because of the storm."

I knew she was interested in me, too, as she asked me, "Where do you live?"

"I live on one of the farms down toward west from Shiprock. I live with my family next to Thomas Yazzie's place." I directed her to the place, too.

"I used to know Thomas and his family when I was very small," she almost cried. "It's always sad to lose friends."

I felt sorry for her losing her friends. Right then I knew she was lonely.

"Where do you live?" I asked, as I looked straight down the lighted road.

She hesitated to answer as if she weren't sure of it. Then she said, "I live about four miles from Shiprock." Then she lowered her head as if she was worried about something I'd said.

I didn't talk any more after that. Again it was quiet. I kept my mind on the road, trying to forget my warm feelings for her beauty.

The night settled itself across the desert land, making stars and the moon more bright. The night sky and the dampness made me sleepy. I felt in a dreamy, romantic mood. The rain still covered the road. It was too quiet for comfort.

"Let's listen to some music," I interrupted the silence as I turned on the radio. I tuned to some rock'n roll music. So now, with the cool night, beating music, and our silence we drove until she asked me to stop. It was just about a mile over two hills to Shiprock. I stopped where a dirt road joined the highway.

"Is this the path to your place?" I quickly asked before she departed.

"Yes. I live about three miles on this road." She pointed her lips for direction as she placed her hand on the door handle.

"I wish I could take you home, but the road is too wet. I might never get home tonight. Well, I hope I'll see you in Shiprock sometime. By the way, what's your name?" I tried to keep her there a while longer by talking to her.

She took a long time to say her name. "Susan Billy," she said finally. Then she added, "Maybe I can visit you some of these nights." She smiled as she opened the door and stepped out of the car.

"All right; good-bye." I tried to show how I felt as I said those last words.

I looked back in the mirror as I dropped over the hill. She stood waving her hand. I felt proud to find someone like her who wanted so much to see me again. I already missed her. Or was she just joking about her visit? Why would she want to visit me at night? I smiled, hoping she'd come very soon.

Before I knew I was home, I stopped at our garage. The lights in the house were out, and the rain had wet the red brick building to a deeper red. I couldn't wait to get into the bed where I could freely think about Susan. I didn't bother to eat or wake my folks. I just covered myself with the warm blankets.

Another sunny morning turned into a cloudy and windy afternoon. Rain clouds brought another chilly breeze as they had two evenings ago when I went to Window Rock. I had not forgotten Susan and, deep in my heart, I kept expecting her visit which she had spoken of. Today, though, we must go to the field to plant new seeds. The cold called for a warm jacket. I glanced around the room where I usually placed my sweater, a maroon-and-gold-colored school sweater. I walked through the house, but I didn't find it. I used my old jacket instead, hoping my sweater was in the car at the hospital where my brother-in-law, Martin, was working.

The movements of my arms and legs, my digging and sowing seeds, were in my usual routine for the last few weeks. I could let my mind wander to Susan while my body went on with its work. Suddenly I remembered offering her my sweater on that trip.

"Are you tired already? What are you thinking about? Supper?" my brother asked when he saw me standing with a smile on my face.

"I remembered where I left my sweater. What time is it?" I asked him, wishing the time for Martin to come home with the pickup were near, but I remembered that our noon lunch wasn't even thought of yet.

"Don't know. I know it's not lunch time yet," he joked, and kept on hoeing the small weeds along the corn rows.

It wasn't until late that evening, about six-thirty, that I was on my way to see Susan. My whole life filled with joy. The dirt road leading off the highway where Susan had stood seemed dried enough for the tires to roll on.

Slowly and very nervously I approached the end of the three miles to her place. I rode over the last hill and stopped at a hogan.

The people were still outside, eating their supper under a shade-house. A familiar man sat facing me from the circle around the dishes on the ground. I was sure I'd seen him someplace, but I couldn't recall where. His wife sat beside him, keeping busy frying some round, thin dough. Three small children accompanied them, two older girls and a child—I couldn't tell whether it was a girl or a boy. I politely asked the man where the Billys lived. He pointed his finger to the west from his cross-legged sitting position. It was at the next hogan where I could find Susan.

"Their hogans are near, over beyond that rocky hill," he directed me in his unmannered way. His words came from his filled mouth.

"They moved to the mountain several days ago," his wife interrupted, "but I saw a light at the place last night. The husband might have ridden down for their supplies."

Hopefully I started again. Sure enough, there were the mud hogans, standing on a lonely plateau. As I approached, a man paused from his busy packing and stood watching me.

He set down a box of groceries and came to the car door. I reached out the window and shook his hand for greeting.

"Hello. Do you know where Susan Billy lives?" I asked, pretending I didn't know where to go to find her.

"Susan Billy?" He looked down, puzzled, and pronounced the name as if he'd never heard it before. After a while of silence, he remarked, "I don't know if you are mistaking for our Susan, or there might be another girl by that name."

My hope almost left as I explained further. "Two nights ago I gave her a ride from Littlewater to the road over there. She told me she lived at this place."

His smile disappeared and a puzzled, odd look took its place.

"See that old hogan over in the distance beyond the three sage-brushes?" He pointed to an old caved-in hogan. "Susan Billy is there," he sadly informed me.

"Good. I'll wait here until she comes back." I sank into the car seat happily, but why was he looking so shocked or worried?

"You don't understand," he went on, explaining, "she died ten years ago and she is buried in that hogan."

At first, I thought it was a joke. I knew how some parents would try to keep their daughters or sons from seeing any strangers. His black hair and light complexion, not so smooth or whitish as Susan's, somehow resembled hers.

Then I knew he was lying. "I loaned her my sweater and I forgot to get it back." I tried to convince him to tell the truth.

He seemed so shocked as he looked more carefully at the old hogan again. "See that red object on one of the logs?" He pointed out that it hadn't been there until recently.

I saw the maroon object. I could instantly recognize my sweater at a distance. My heart almost stopped with the horrible shock. I struggled to catch my breath back. I didn't believe in ghosts until then, but I had to believe my sweater. I had to believe the beautiful girl who had ridden with me, who had promised to visit me. Still, why hadn't she killed me like the rest of her victims? Was it because of my sweater or because of the love we shared?

From that day, I had proven to myself the truth of the Navaho superstitions. I know I shall never get my sweater back, but on one of these windy nights, I will see Susan again as she promised. What will I do then?

FOR DISCUSSION

1. How does the author prepare you, at the beginning of the story, for a supernatural occurrence? What is the main character's reaction to this phenomenon?

2. Compare the treatment of the supernatural in this story to that in "Summer Water and Shirley." How are they alike? How are they different?

Littlebird

b. 1951

Littlebird is a full-blooded Indian of Santo Domingo and Laguna tribal descent. Born in Albuquerque, New Mexico, he attended public schools in Oakland, California, and in Brigham City, Utah. From grades nine through twelve, he was a student at the Institute of American Indian Arts, from which he was graduated in 1969.

Death in the Woods

Corn swaying in the rhythm of the wind —
  Graceful ballerinas,
  Emerging at the edge of the forest.

All dip and dance;
  Wind tunnels through long silken hair,
  Golden teeth-seeds.

Trees chatter nervously
  Awakening sky in fright,
  Pointing at Woodman.

A mighty thud! Blow leaves deep scar;
  He strikes again . . . .

117

Corn mourns golden tears,
    Bows, praying for fallen brother.

Jay mocks the greedy beast
    Who has doomed majestic brother,
    His life home.

Wind tosses leaves aside as
    Woodman tramps on his way,
    Ax dripping Oak's blood.

The forest, damp and silent,
    Mourning for lost Oak.
    And now remains but a
    Chirp of a lonely cricket and
    Silhouette of Woodman,
    Diminishing,
        beyond the
            saddened hill
                as the far
                    sun sinks.

FOR DISCUSSION

Describe the action in the poem. How do the creatures of nature react toward Oak and Woodman? Do you think Woodman is a part of nature too?

N. Scott Momaday

b. 1934

Winner of the 1969 Pulitzer Prize for Fiction for his novel House Made of Dawn, *of which this selection forms a part, N. Scott Momaday is on the English faculty at Stanford University. The son of an artist father, Al Momaday, and an author-artist mother, Natachee Scott Momaday, he is of Kiowa and Cherokee descent. Born in Lawton, Oklahoma, he grew up on Navaho, Apache, and Pueblo reservations throughout the Southwest.*

Mr. Momaday earned his A. B. degree from the University of New Mexico and received his master's and doctoral degrees from Stanford. He has taught at both the Santa Barbara and Berkeley campuses of the University of California. Among his other works are The Way to Rainy Mountain *(1969) and* Angle of Geese and Other Poems *(1973). His poems have appeared in numerous magazines and anthologies.*

The Bear and the Colt

He was a young man, and he rode out on the buckskin colt to the north and west, leading the hunting horse, across the river and beyond the white cliffs and the plain, beyond the hills and the mesas, the canyons and the caves. And once, where the horses could not go because the face of the rock was almost vertical and unbroken and the ancient handholds were worn away to shadows in the centuries of wind and rain, he climbed among the walls and pinnacles of rock, adhering like a vine to the face of the rock, pressing with no force at all his whole mind and weight upon the sheer ascent, running the roots of his weight into invisible hollows and cracks, and he heard the whistle and moan of the wind among the crags, like ancient voices, and saw the horses far below in the sunlit gorge. And there were the caves. He came suddenly upon a narrow ledge and stood before the mouth of a cave. It was sealed with silver webs, and he brushed them away. He bent to enter and knelt down on the floor. It was dark and cool and close inside, and smelled of damp earth and dead and ancient fires, as if centuries ago the air had entered and stood still behind the web. The dead embers and ashes lay still in a mound upon the floor, and the floor was deep and packed with clay and glazed with the blood of animals. The chiseled dome was low and encrusted with smoke, and the one round wall was a perfect radius of rock and plaster. Here and there were earthen bowls, one very large, chipped and broken only at the mouth, deep and fired within. It was beautiful and thin-shelled and fragile-looking, but he struck the nails of his hand against it, and it rang like metal. There was a black metate[1] by the door, the coarse, igneous[2] grain of the shallow bowl forever bleached with meal, and in the ashes of the fire were several ears and cobs of corn, each no bigger than his thumb, charred and brittle, but whole and hard as wood. And there among the things of the dead he listened in the stillness all around and heard only the lowing of the wind . . . and then the plummet and rush of a great swooping bird—out of the corner of his eye he saw the awful shadow which hurtled across the light—and the clatter of wings on the cliff, and the small, thin cry of a rodent. And in the same instant the huge wings heaved with calm, gathering up the dead weight, and rose away.

All afternoon he rode on toward the summit of the blue mountain, and at last he was high among the falls and the steep timbered slopes. The sun fell behind the land above him and the dusk grew up among the trees, and still he went on in the dying light, climbing up to the top of the land. And all afternoon he had seen the tracks of wild animals and heard the motion of the dead leaves and the breaking of branches on either side. Twice he had seen

---

[1] METATE (mə•täd´ē): stone used for grinding corn and other grains.
[2] IGNEOUS (ĭg´nē•əs): formed from previously molten rock.

deer, motionless, watching, standing away in easy range, blended with light and shadow, fading away into the leaves and the land. He let them be, but remembered where they were and how they stood, reckoning well and instinctively their notion of fear and flight, their age and weight.

He had seen the tracks of wolves and mountain lions and the deep prints of a half-grown bear, and in the last light he drew up in a small clearing and made his camp. It was a good place, and he was lucky to have come upon it while he still could see. A dead tree had fallen upon a bed of rock; it was clear of the damp earth and the leaves, and the wood made an almost smokeless fire. The timber all around was thick, and it held the light and the sound of the fire within the clearing. He tethered the horses there in the open, as close to the fire as he could, and opened the blanket roll and ate. He slept sitting against the saddle, and kept the fire going and the rifle cocked across his waist.

He awoke startled to the stiffening of the horses. They stood quivering and taut with their heads high and turned around upon the dark and nearest wall of trees. He could see the whites of their eyes and the ears laid back upon the bristling manes and the almost imperceptible shiver and bunch of their haunches to the spine. And at the same time he saw the dark shape sauntering among the trees, and then the others, sitting all around, motionless, the short pointed ears and the soft shining eyes, almost kindly and discreet, the gaze of the gray heads bidding only welcome and wild good will. And he was young and it was the first time he had come among them and he brought the rifle up and made no sound. He swung the sights slowly around from one to another of the still, shadowy shapes, but they made no sign except to cock their heads a notch, sitting still and away in the darkness like a litter of pups, full of shyness and wonder and delight. He was hard on the track of the bear; it was somewhere close by in the night, and it knew of him, had been ahead of him for hours in the afternoon and evening, holding the same methodical pace, unhurried, certain of where it was and where he was and of every step of the way between, keeping always and barely out of sight, almost out of hearing. And it was there now, off in the blackness, standing still and invisible, waiting. And he did not want to break the stillness of the night, for it was holy and profound; it was rest and restoration, the hunter's offering of death and the sad watch of the hunted, waiting somewhere away in the cold darkness and breathing easily of its life, brooding around at last to forgiveness and consent; the silence was essential to them both, and it lay out like a bond between them, ancient and inviolable. He could neither take nor give any advantage of cowardice where no cowardice was, and he laid the rifle down. He spoke low to the horses and soothed them. He drew fresh wood upon the fire and the gray shapes crept away to the edge of the light, and in the morning they were gone.

It was gray before the dawn and there was a thin frost on the leaves, and he saddled up and started out again, slowly, after the track and into the wind. At sunrise he came upon the ridge of the mountain. For hours he followed the ridge, and he could see for miles across the land. It was late in the autumn and clear, and the great shining slopes, green and blue, rose out of the shadows on either side, and the sunlit groves of aspen shone bright with clusters of yellow leaves and thin white lines of bark, and far below in the deep folds of the land he could see the tops of the black pines swaying. At midmorning he was low in a saddle of the ridge, and he came upon a huge outcrop of rock, and the track was lost. An ancient watercourse fell away like a flight of stairs to the left, the falls broad and shallow at first, but ever more narrow and deep farther down. He tied the horses and started down the rock on foot, using the rifle to balance himself. He went slowly, quietly down until he came to a deep open funnel in the rock. The ground on either side sloped sharply down to a broad ravine and the edge of the timber beyond, and he saw the scored earth where the bear had left the rock and gone sliding down, and the swath in the brush of the ravine. He thought of going the same way; it would be quick and easy, and he was close to the kill, closing in and growing restless. But he must make no sound of hurry. The bear knew he was coming, knew better than he how close he was, was even now watching him from the wood, waiting, but still he must make no sound of hurry. The walls of the funnel were deep and smooth, and they converged at the bank of the ravine some twenty feet below, and the ravine was filled with sweet clover and paintbrush[3] and sage. He held the rifle out as far as he could reach and let it go; it fell upon a stand of tall sweet clover with scarcely any sound, and the dull stock shone and the long barrel glinted among

[3] PAINTBRUSH: plant with colorful, tufted flowers.

the curving green and yellow stalks. He let himself down into the
funnel, little by little, supported only by the tension of his strength
against the walls. The going was hard and slow, and near the end
his arms and legs began to shake, but he was young and strong,
and he dropped from the point of the rock to the sand below and
took up the rifle and went on, not hurrying but going only as fast
as the bear had gone, going even in the bear's tracks, across the
ravine and up the embankment and through the trees, unwary now,
sensible only of closing in, going on and looking down at the tracks.

And when at last he looked up, the timber stood around a pool
of light, and the bear was standing still and small at the far side
of the brake, careless, unheeding. He brought the rifle up, and the
bear raised and turned its head and made no sign of fear. It was
small and black in the deep shade and dappled with light, its body
turned three-quarters away and standing perfectly still, and the
flat head and the small black eyes that were fixed upon him hung
around upon the shoulder and under the hump of the spine. The
bear was young and heavy with tallow, and the underside of the
body and the backs of its short, thick legs were tufted with winter
hair, longer and lighter than the rest, and dull as dust. His hand
tightened on the stock and the rifle bucked and the sharp report
rang upon the walls and carried out upon the slopes, and he heard
the sudden scattering of birds overhead and saw the darting shadows all around. The bullet slammed into the flesh and jarred the
whole black body once, but the head remained motionless and the
eyes level upon him. Then, and for one instant only, there was
a sad and meaningless haste. The bear turned away and lumbered,
though not with fear, not with any hurt, but haste, slightly reflex-
ive, a single step, or two, or three, and it was overcome. It shud-
dered and looked around again and fell.

The hunt was over, and only then could he hurry; it was over
and well done. The wound was small and clean, behind the foreleg
and low on the body, where the fur and flesh were thin, and there
was no blood at the mouth. He took out his pouch of pollen and
made yellow streaks above the bear's eyes. It was almost noon,
and he hurried. He disemboweled the bear and laid the flesh open
with splints so that the blood should not run into the fur and stain
the hide. He ate quickly of the bear's liver,[4] taking it with him,

---

[4] ATE . . . LIVER: that is, to acquire the animal's strength.

thinking what he must do, remembering now his descent upon the rock and the whole lay of the land, all the angles of his vision from the ridge. He went quickly, a quarter of a mile or more down the ravine, until he came to a place where the horses could keep their footing on the near side of the ridge. The blood of the bear was on him, and the bear's liver was warm and wet in his hand. He came upon the ridge, and the colt grew wild in its eyes and blew, pulling away, and its hoofs clattered on the rock and the skin crawled at the roots of its mane. He approached it slowly, talking to it, and took hold of the reins. The hunting horse watched, full of age and indifference, switching its tail. There was no time to lose. He held hard to the reins, turning down the bit in the colt's mouth, and his voice rose a little and was edged. Slowly he brought the bear's flesh up to the flaring nostrils of the colt and smeared the muzzle with it.

And he rode the colt back down the mountain, leading the hunting horse with the bear on its back, and, like the old hunting horse and the young black bear, he and the colt had come of age and were hunters, too. He made camp that night far down in the peneplain[5] and saw the stars and heard the coyotes away by the river. And in the early morning he rode into the town. He was a man then, and smeared with the blood of a bear. He shouted, and the men came out to meet him. They came with rifles, and he gave them strips of the bear's flesh, which they wrapped around the barrels of their guns. And soon the women came with switches, and they spoke to the bear and laid the switches to its hide. The men and women were jubilant and all around, and he rode stone-faced in their midst, looking straight ahead.

[5] PENEPLAIN (pē′nə•plān): nearly flat land surface in an advanced stage of erosion.

FOR DISCUSSION

1. What hints is the reader given at the beginning of the story that the killing of the bear has deeper significance than the mere acquisition of meat and fur?

2. What does Momaday mean when he writes, ". . . like the old hunting horse and the young black bear, he and the colt had come of age and were hunters, too"?

FROM
The Way to Rainy Mountain

A single knoll rises out of the plain in Oklahoma, north and west of the Wichita Range. For my people, the Kiowas, it is an old landmark, and they gave it the name Rainy Mountain. The hardest weather in the world is there. Winter brings blizzards, hot tornadic winds arise in the spring, and in summer the prairie is an anvil's edge. The grass turns brittle and brown, and it cracks beneath your feet. There are green belts along the rivers and creeks, linear groves of hickory and pecan, willow and witch hazel. At a distance in July or August the steaming foliage seems almost to writhe in fire. Great green-and-yellow grasshoppers are everywhere in the tall grass, popping up like corn to sting the flesh, and tortoises crawl about on the red earth, going nowhere in the plenty of time. Loneliness is an aspect of the land. All things in the plain are isolate; there is no confusion of objects in the eye, but *one* hill or *one* tree or *one* man. To look upon that landscape in the early morning, with the sun at your back, is to lose the sense of proportion. Your imagination comes to life, and this, you think, is where Creation was begun.

I returned to Rainy Mountain in July. My grandmother had died in the spring, and I wanted to be at her grave. She had lived to be very old and at last infirm. Her only living daughter was with her when she died, and I was told that in death her face was that of a child.

I like to think of her as a child. When she was born, the Kiowas were living that last great moment of their history. For more than a hundred years they had controlled the open range from the Smoky Hill River to the Red, from the headwaters of the Canadian to the fork of the Arkansas and Cimarron. In alliance with the Comanches, they had ruled the whole of the southern Plains. War was their sacred business, and they were among the finest horsemen the world has ever known. But warfare for the Kiowas was preeminently a matter of disposition rather than of survival, and they never understood the grim, unrelenting advance of the U.S. Cavalry. When at last, divided and ill-provisioned, they were driven onto the Staked Plains in the cold rains of autumn, they fell into panic. In Palo Duro Canyon they abandoned their crucial stores to pillage and had nothing then but their lives. In order to save themselves, they surrendered to the soldiers at Fort Sill and were imprisoned in the old stone corral that now stands as a military museum. My grandmother was spared the humiliation of those high gray walls by eight or ten years, but she must have known from birth the affliction of defeat, the dark brooding of old warriors.

Her name was Aho, and she belonged to the last culture to evolve in North America. Her forebears came down from the high country in western Montana nearly three centuries ago. They were a mountain people, a mysterious tribe of hunters whose language has never been positively classified in any major group. In the late seventeenth century they began a long migration to the south and east. It was a journey toward the dawn, and it led to a golden age. Along the way the Kiowas were befriended by the Crows, who gave them the culture and religion of the Plains. They acquired horses, and their ancient nomadic spirit was suddenly free of the ground. They acquired Tai-me, the sacred Sun Dance[1] doll, from that moment the object and symbol of their worship, and so shared in the divinity of the sun. Not least, they acquired the sense of destiny, therefore courage and pride. When they entered upon the southern Plains, they had been transformed. No longer were they slaves to the simple necessity of survival; they were a lordly and dangerous society of fighters and thieves, hunters and priests of the sun. According to their origin myth, they entered the world through a hollow log. From one point of view, their migration was the fruit of an old prophecy, for indeed they emerged from a sunless world.

Although my grandmother lived out her long life in the shadow of Rainy Mountain, the immense landscape of the continental interior lay like memory in her blood. She could tell of the Crows, whom she had never seen, and of the Black Hills, where she had never been. I wanted to see in reality what she had seen more perfectly in the mind's eye, and traveled fifteen hundred miles to begin my pilgrimage.

[1] Sun Dance: important religious ceremony among Plains Indian tribes, usually performed in the summer to influence the elements of nature, and requiring extraordinary endurance of the dancers.

Yellowstone, it seemed to me, was the top of the world, a region of deep lakes and dark timber, canyons and waterfalls. But, beautiful as it is, one might have the sense of confinement there. The skyline in all directions is close at hand, the high wall of the woods and deep cleavages of shade. There is a perfect freedom in the mountains, but it belongs to the eagle and the elk, the badger and the bear. The Kiowas reckoned their stature by the distance they could see, and they were bent and blind in the wilderness.

Descending eastward, the highland meadows are a stairway to the plain. In July the inland slope of the Rockies is luxuriant with flax and buckwheat, stonecrop and larkspur. The earth unfolds and the limit of the land recedes. Clusters of trees and animals grazing far in the distance cause the vision to reach away and wonder to build upon the mind. The sun follows a longer course in the day, and the sky is immense beyond all comparison. The great billowing clouds that sail upon it are shadows that move upon the grain like water, dividing light. Farther down, in the land of the Crows and Blackfeet, the plain is yellow. Sweet clover takes hold of the hills and bends upon itself to cover and seal the soil. There the Kiowas paused on their way; they had come to the place where they must change their lives. The sun is at home on the plains. Precisely there does it have the certain character of a god. When the Kiowas came to the land of the Crows, they could see the dark lees of the hills at dawn across the Bighorn River, the profusion of light on the grain shelves, the oldest deity ranging after the solstices. Not yet would they veer southward to the caldron of the land that lay below; they must wean their blood from the northern winter and hold the mountains a while longer in their view. They bore Tai-me in procession to the east.

A dark mist lay over the Black Hills, and the land was like iron. At the top of a ridge I caught sight of Devil's Tower upthrust against the gray sky as if in the birth of time the core of the earth had broken through its crust and the motion of the world was begun. There are things in nature that engender an awful quiet in the heart of man; Devil's Tower is one of them. Two centuries ago, because they could not do otherwise, the Kiowas made a legend at the base of the rock. My grandmother said:

> "Eight children were there at play, seven sisters and
> their brother. Suddenly the boy was struck dumb; he

trembled and began to run upon his hands and feet. His fingers became claws, and his body was covered with fur. Directly there was a bear where the boy had been. The sisters were terrified; they ran, and the bear after them. They came to the stump of a great tree, and the tree spoke to them. It bade them climb upon it, and as they did so, it began to rise into the air. The bear came to kill them, but they were just beyond its reach. It reared against the tree and scored the bark all around with its claws. The seven sisters were borne into the sky, and they became the stars of the Big Dipper."

From that moment, and so long as the legend lives, the Kiowas have kinsmen in the night sky. Whatever they were in the mountains, they could be no more. However tenuous their well-being, however much they had suffered and would suffer again, they had found a way out of the wilderness.

My grandmother had a reverence for the sun, a holy regard that now is all but gone out of mankind. There was a wariness in her, and an ancient awe. She was a Christian in her later years, but she had come a long way about, and she never forgot her birthright. As a child she had been to the Sun Dances; she had taken part in those annual rites, and by them she had learned the restoration of her people in the presence of Tai-me. She was about seven when the last Kiowa Sun Dance was held in 1887 on the Washita River above Rainy Mountain Creek. The buffalo were gone. In order to consummate the ancient sacrifice—to impale the head of a buffalo bull upon the medicine tree—a delegation of old men journeyed into Texas, there to beg and barter for an animal from the Goodnight herd. She was ten when the Kiowas came together for the last time as a living Sun Dance culture. They could find no buffalo; they had to hang an old hide from the sacred tree. Before the dance could begin, a company of soldiers rode out from Fort Sill under orders to disperse the tribe. Forbidden without cause the essential act of their faith, having seen the wild herds slaughtered and left to rot upon the ground, the Kiowas backed away forever from the medicine tree. That was July 20, 1890, at the great bend of the Washita. My grandmother was there. Without bitterness, and for as long as she lived, she bore a vision of deicide.

Now that I can have her only in memory, I see my grandmother in the several postures that were peculiar to her: standing at the wood stove on a winter morning and turning meat in a great iron skillet; sitting at the south window, bent above her beadwork, and afterwards, when her vision failed, looking down for a long time into the fold of her hands; going out upon a cane, very slowly as she did when the weight of age came upon her; praying. I remember her most often at prayer. She made long, rambling prayers out of suffering and hope, having seen many things. I was never sure that I had the right to hear, so exclusive were they of all mere custom and company. The last time I saw her she prayed standing by the side of her bed at night, naked to the waist, the light of a kerosene lamp moving upon her dark skin. Her long, black hair, always drawn and braided in the day, lay upon her shoulders and against her breasts like a shawl. I do not speak Kiowa, and I never understood her prayers, but there was something inherently sad in the sound, some merest hesitation upon the syllables of sorrow. She began in a high and descending pitch, exhausting her breath to silence; then again and again—and always the same intensity of effort, of something that is, and is not, like urgency in the human voice. Transported so in the dancing light among the shadows of her room, she seemed beyond the reach of time. But that was illusion; I think I knew then that I should not see her again.

Houses are like sentinels in the plain, old keepers of the weather watch. There, in a very little while, wood takes on the appearance of great age. All colors wear soon away in the wind and rain, and then the wood is burned gray and the grain appears and the nails turn red with rust. The windowpanes are black and opaque; you imagine there is nothing within, and indeed there are many ghosts, bones given up to the land. They stand here and there against the sky, and you approach them for a longer time than you expect. They belong in the distance; it is their domain.

Once there was a lot of sound in my grandmother's house, a lot of coming and going, feasting and talk. The summers there were full of excitement and reunion. The Kiowas are a summer people; they abide the cold and keep to themselves; but when the season turns and the land becomes warm and vital, they cannot hold still; an old love of going returns upon them. The aged visitors who came to my grandmother's house when I was a child were made of lean and leather, and they bore themselves upright. They wore great black hats and bright ample shirts that shook in the wind. They rubbed fat upon their hair and wound their braids with strips of colored cloth. Some of them painted their faces and carried the scars of old and cherished enmities. They were an old council of warlords, come to remind and be reminded of who they were. Their wives and daughters served them well. The women might indulge themselves; gossip was at once the mark and compensation of their servitude. They made loud and elaborate talk among themselves, full of jest and gesture, fright and false alarm. They went abroad in fringed and flowered shawls, bright beadwork and German silver. They were at home in the kitchen, and they prepared meals that were banquets.

There were frequent prayer meetings, and great nocturnal feasts. When I was a child, I played with my cousins outside, where the lamplight fell upon the ground and the singing of the old people rose up around us and carried away into the darkness. There were a lot of good things to eat, a lot of laughter and surprise. And afterwards, when the quiet returned, I lay down with my grandmother and could hear the frogs away by the river and feel the motion of the air.

Now there is a funeral silence in the rooms, the endless wake of some final word. The walls have closed in upon my grandmother's house. When I returned to it in mourning, I saw for the first time in my life how small it was. It was late at night, and there was a white moon, nearly full. I sat for a long time on the stone steps by the kitchen door. From there I could see out across the land; I could see the long row of trees by the creek, the low light upon the rolling plains, and the stars of the Big Dipper. Once I looked at the moon and caught sight of a strange thing. A cricket had perched upon the handrail, only a few inches away from me. My line of vision was such that the creature filled the moon like a fossil. It had gone there, I thought, to live and die, for there, of all places, was its small definition made whole and eternal. A warm wind rose up and purled like the longing within me.

The next morning I awoke at dawn and went out on the dirt road to Rainy Mountain. It was already hot, and the grasshoppers began to fill the air. Still, it was early in the morning, and the birds sang out of the shadows. The long yellow grass on the mountain shone in the bright light, and a scissortail[2] hied above the land. There, where it ought to be, at the end of a long and legendary way, was my grandmother's grave. Here and there on the dark stones were ancestral names. Looking back once, I saw the mountain and came away.

[2] SCISSORTAIL: bird with a long, forked tail.

FOR DISCUSSION

1. Why does the author say that his grandmother's grave was "where it ought to be, at the end of a long and legendary way. . ."?

2. How does Momaday relate the evolution of the Kiowa people to their migration to the south and east?

James Welch

b. 1940

Born a Blackfeet Indian in Browning, Montana, James Welch received his undergraduate degree in liberal arts from the University of Montana. He now pursues writing on a full-time basis.

Mr. Welch's poems have appeared in many anthologies and magazines. Riding the Earthboy 40, *his first poetry collection, came out in 1971 and* Winter in the Blood, *his first novel, in 1974. Like Momaday, he is considered a poet of unusual distinction.*

The Man from Washington

The end came easy for most of us.
Packed away in our crude beginnings
in some far corner of a flat world,
we didn't expect much more
than firewood and buffalo robes
to keep us warm. The man came down,
a slouching dwarf with rainwater eyes,
and spoke to us. He promised
that life would go on as usual,
that treaties would be signed, and everyone—
man, woman, and child—would be innoculated
against a world in which we had no part,
a world of wealth, promise, and fabulous disease.

FOR DISCUSSION

What is the tone of this poem? Discuss its effectiveness.

Vine Deloria, Jr.

b. 1933

One of the most articulate contemporary spokesmen for Red Power, Vine Deloria feels that Indians must no longer accept the myths the public at large accords to them. "It is up to us [Indians] to write the final chapter of the American Indian upon this continent." Born a Standing Rock Sioux on Pine Ridge Reservation in South Dakota, he is the son of Episcopalian minister Vine Deloria. He studied at Iowa State University, served in the Marine Corps, and was graduated from the Lutheran School of Theology.

From 1964 to 1967 Mr. Deloria served as executive director of the National Congress of American Indians. He left that post to attend the University of Colorado Law School, feeling that a legal education was the best way to establish "our own legal program for defense of Indian treaty rights." After his legal studies he taught at Western Washington State College before becoming chairman of the Institute for Development of Indian Law in Washington, D.C.

Mr. Deloria is the author of numerous magazine articles. Among his recent books are God Is Red *(1973) and* Behind the Trail of Broken Treaties *(1974).*

This Country Was a Lot Better Off When the Indians Were Running It

On November 9, 1969, a contingent of American Indians, led by Adam Nordwall, a Chippewa from Minnesota, and Richard Oakes, a Mohawk from New York, landed on Alcatraz Island in San Francisco Bay and claimed the thirteen-acre rock "by right of discovery." The island had been abandoned six and a half years ago, and

133

although there had been various suggestions concerning its disposal, nothing had been done to make use of the land. Since there are Federal treaties giving some tribes the right to abandoned Federal property within a tribe's original territory, the Indians of the Bay area felt that they could lay claim to the island.

For nearly a year the United Bay Area Council of American Indians, a confederation of urban Indian organizations, had been talking about submitting a bid for the island to use it as a West Coast Indian cultural center and vocational training headquarters. Then, on November 1, the San Francisco American Indian Center burned down. The center had served an estimated thirty thousand Indians in the immediate area and was the focus of activities of the urban Indian community. It became a matter of urgency after that, and as Adam Nordwall said, "It was GO." Another landing on November 20, by nearly one hundred Indians in a swift midnight raid, secured the island.

The new inhabitants have made "the Rock" a focal point symbolic of Indian people. Under extreme difficulty they have worked to begin repairing sanitary facilities and buildings. The population has been largely transient; many people have stopped by, looked the situation over for a few days, then gone home, unwilling to put in the tedious work necessary to make the island support a viable community.

The Alcatraz news stories are somewhat shocking to non-Indians. It is difficult for most Americans to comprehend that there still exists a living community of nearly one million Indians in this country. For many people, Indians have become a species of movie actor periodically dispatched to the Happy Hunting Grounds by John Wayne on the "Late, Late Show." Yet there are some 315 Indian tribal groups in twenty-six states still functioning as quasi-sovereign nations under treaty status; they range from the mammoth Navaho tribe of some 132,000 with sixteen million acres of land to tiny Mission Creek of California with 15 people and a tiny parcel of property. There are over half a million Indians in the cities alone, with the largest concentrations in San Francisco, Los Angeles, Minneapolis, and Chicago.

The take-over of Alcatraz is to many Indian people a demonstration of pride in being Indian and a dignified, yet humorous, protest against current conditions existing on the reservations and in the cities. It is this special pride and dignity, the determination to judge life according to one's own values and the unconquerable conviction that the tribes will not die, that has always characterized Indian people as I have known them.

I was born in Martin, a border town on the Pine Ridge Indian Reservation in South Dakota, in the midst of the depression.[1] My father was an Indian missionary who served eighteen chapels on the eastern half of the reservation. In 1934, when I was one, the Indian Reorganization Act was passed, allowing Indian tribes full rights of self-government for the first time since the late 1860s. Ever since those days, when the Sioux had agreed to forsake the life of the hunter for that of the farmer, they had been systematically deprived of any voice in decisions affecting their lives and property. Tribal ceremonies and religious practices were forbidden. The reservation was fully controlled by men in Washington, most of whom had never visited a reservation and felt no urge to do so.

The first years on the reservations were extremely hard for the Sioux. Kept confined behind fences, they were almost wholly dependent upon Government rations for their food supply. Many died of hunger and malnutrition. Game was scarce, and few were allowed to have weapons for fear of another Indian war. In some years there was practically no food available. Other years rations were withheld until the men agreed to farm the tiny pieces of land each family had been given. In desperation many families were forced to eat stray dogs and cats to keep alive.

By World War I, however, many of the Sioux families had developed prosperous ranches. Then the Government stepped in, sold the Indians' cattle for wartime needs, and after the war leased the grazing land to whites, creating wealthy white ranchers and destitute Indian landlords.

With the passage of the Indian Reorganization Act, native ceremonies and practices were given full recognition by Federal authorities. My earliest memories are of trips along dusty roads to Kyle, a small settlement in the heart of the reservation, to attend the dances. Ancient men, veterans of battles even then considered footnotes to the settlement of the West, brought their costumes out of hiding and walked about the grounds gathering the honors

[1] DEPRESSION: period of decline in the national economy, which began in 1929.

they had earned half a century before. They danced as if the intervening fifty years had been a lost weekend from which they had
fully recovered. I remember best Dewey Beard, then in his late
eighties and a survivor of the Little Bighorn. Even at that late
date Dewey was hesitant to speak of the battle for fear of reprisal.
There was no doubt, as one watched the people's expressions, that
the Sioux had survived their greatest ordeal and were ready to
face whatever the future might bring.

In those days the reservation was isolated and unsettled. Dirt
roads held the few mail routes together. One could easily get lost
in the wild back country as roads turned into cowpaths without
so much as a backward glance. Remote settlements such as Buzzard
Basin and Cuny Table were nearly inaccessible. In the spring every
bridge on the reservation would be washed out with the first rain
and would remain out until late summer. But few people cared.
Most of the reservation people, traveling by team and wagon,
merely forded the creeks and continued their journey, almost con-
temptuous of the need for roads and bridges.

The most memorable event of my early childhood was visiting
Wounded Knee where two hundred Sioux, including women and
children, were slaughtered in 1890 by troopers of the Seventh
Cavalry in what is believed to have been a delayed act of ven-
geance for Custer's defeat. The people were simply lined up and
shot down much as was allegedly done, according to newspaper
reports, at Songmy.[2] The wounded were left to die in a three-day
Dakota blizzard, and when the soldiers returned to the scene after
the storm, some were still alive and were saved. The massacre was
vividly etched in the minds of many of the older reservation people, but it was difficult to find anyone who wanted to talk about it.

Many times, over the years, my father would point out survivors
of the massacre, and people on the reservation always went out
of their way to help them. For a long time there was a bill in Congress to pay indemnities to the survivors, but the War Department
always insisted that it had been a "battle" to stamp out the Ghost
Dance religion among the Sioux. This does not, however, explain
bayoneted Indian women and children found miles from the scene
of the incident.

[2] SONGMY: also known as My Lai Four, a village in South Vietnam where hundreds
of civilians were reportedly shot by American infantrymen in March, 1968.

Strangely enough, the depression was good for Indian reservations, particularly for the people at Pine Ridge. Since their lands had been leased to non-Indians by the Bureau of Indian Affairs, they had only a small rent check and the contempt of those who leased their lands to show for their ownership. But the Federal programs devised to solve the national economic crisis were also made available to Indian people, and there was work available for the first time in the history of the reservations.

The Civilian Conservation Corps[3] set up a camp on the reservation, and many Indians were hired under the program. In the canyons north of Allen, South Dakota, a beautiful buffalo pasture was built by the CCC, and the whole area was transformed into a recreation wonderland. Indians would come from miles around to see the buffalo and leave with a strange look in their eyes. Many times I stood silently watching while old men talked to the buffalo about the old days. They would conclude by singing a song before respectfully departing, their eyes filled with tears and their minds occupied with the memories of other times and places. It was difficult to determine who was the captive—the buffalo fenced in or the Indian fenced out.

While the rest of America suffered from the temporary deprivation of its luxuries, Indian people had a period of prosperity, as it were. Paychecks were regular. Small cattle herds were started; cars were purchased; new clothes and necessities became available. To a people who had struggled along on fifty dollars cash income per year, the CCC was the greatest program ever to come along. The Sioux had climbed from absolute deprivation to mere poverty, and this was the best time the reservation ever had.

World War II ended this temporary prosperity. The CCC camps were closed, reservation programs were cut to the bone, and social services became virtually non-existent; victory gardens[4] were suddenly the style, and people began to be aware that a great war was being waged overseas.

The war dispersed the reservation people as nothing ever had. Every day, it seemed, we would be bidding farewell to families

[3] CIVILIAN CONSERVATION CORPS: Federal agency which hired unemployed young men for public conservation work in the 1930s.

[4] VICTORY GARDENS: homeowners' personal gardens cultivated during World War II to increase food production.

as they headed west to work in the defense plants on the Coast.

A great number of Sioux people went west, and many of the Sioux on Alcatraz today are their children and relatives. There may now be as many Sioux in California as there are on the reservations in South Dakota because of the great wartime migration.

Those who stayed on the reservation had the war brought directly to their doorstep when they were notified that their sons had to go across the seas and fight. Busloads of Sioux boys left the reservation for parts unknown. In many cases even the trip to nearby Martin was a new experience for them, let alone training in Texas, California, or Colorado. There were always going-away ceremonies conducted by the older people who admonished the boys to uphold the old tribal traditions and not to fear death. It was not death they feared but living with an unknown people in a distant place.

I was always disappointed with the Government's way of handling Indian servicemen. Indians were simply lost in the shuffle of three million men in uniform. Many boys came home on furlough and feared to return. They were not cowards in any sense of the word, but the loneliness and boredom of stateside duty was crushing their spirits. They spent months without seeing another Indian. If the Government had recruited all-Indian outfits, it would have easily solved this problem and also had the best fighting units in the world at its disposal. I often wonder what an all-Sioux or Apache company, painted and singing its songs, would have done to the morale of élite German panzer units.[5]

After the war Indian veterans straggled back to the reservations and tried to pick up their lives. It was very difficult for them to resume a life of poverty after having seen the affluent outside world. Some spent a few days with the old folks and then left again for the big cities. Over the years they have emerged as leaders of the urban Indian movement. Many of their children are the nationalists of today who are adamant about keeping the reservations they have visited only on vacations. Other veterans stayed on the reservations and entered tribal politics.

The reservations radically changed after the war. During the depression there were about five telephones in Martin. If there was a call for you, the man at the hardware store had to come

[5] PANZER UNITS: armored-tank units.

down to your house and get you to answer it. A couple of years after the war a complete dial system was installed that extended to most of the smaller communities on the reservation. Families that had been hundreds of miles from any form of communication were now only minutes away from a telephone.

Roads were built connecting the major communities of the Pine Ridge country. No longer did it take hours to go from one place to another. With these kinds of roads everyone had to have a car. The team and wagon vanished, except for those families who lived at various "camps" in inaccessible canyons pretty much as their ancestors had. (Today, even they have adopted the automobile for traveling long distances in search of work.)

I left the reservation in 1951, when my family moved to Iowa. I went back only once for an extended stay, in the summer of 1955, while on a furlough, and after that I visited only occasionally during summer vacations. In the meantime I attended college, served a hitch in the Marines, and went to the seminary. After I graduated from the seminary, I took a job with the United Scholarship Service, a private organization devoted to the college and secondary-school education of American Indian and Mexican students. I had spent my last two years of high school in an Eastern preparatory school and so was probably the only Indian my age who knew what an independent Eastern school was like. As the program developed, we soon had some thirty students placed in Eastern schools.

I insisted that all the students who entered the program be able to qualify for scholarships as students and not simply as Indians. I was pretty sure we could beat the white man at his own educational game, which seemed to me the only way to gain his respect. I was soon to find that this was a dangerous attitude to have. The very people who were supporting the program—non-Indians in the national church establishments—accused me of trying to form a colonialist "élite" by insisting that only kids with strong test scores and academic patterns be sent east to school. They wanted to continue the ancient pattern of soft-hearted paternalism toward Indians. I didn't feel we should cry our way into the schools, that sympathy would destroy the students we were trying to help.

In 1964, while attending the annual convention of the National Congress of American Indians, I was elected its executive director. I learned more about life in the NCAI in three years than I had in the previous thirty. Every conceivable problem that could occur in an Indian society was suddenly thrust at me from 315 different directions. I discovered that I was one of the people who were supposed to solve the problems. The only trouble was that Indian people locally and on the national level were being played off one against the other by clever whites who had either ego or income at stake. While there were many feasible solutions, few could be tried without whites with vested interests working night and day to destroy the unity we were seeking on a national basis.

In the mid-nineteen-sixties, the whole generation that had grown up after World War II and had left the reservations during the fifties to get an education was returning to Indian life as "educated Indians." But we soon knew better. Tribal societies had existed for centuries without going outside themselves for education and information. Yet many of us thought that we would be able to improve the traditional tribal methods. We were wrong.

For three years we ran around the conference circuit attending numerous meetings called to "solve" the Indian problems. We listened to and spoke with anthropologists, historians, sociologists, psychologists, economists, educators, and missionaries. We worked with many Government agencies and with every conceivable doctrine, idea, and program ever created. At the end of this happy round of consultations the reservation people were still plodding along on their own time schedule, doing the things they considered important. They continued to solve their problems their way in spite of the advice given them by "Indian experts."

By 1967 there was a radical change in thinking on the part of many of us. Conferences were proving unproductive. Where non-Indians had been pushed out to make room for Indian people, they had wormed their way back into power and again controlled the major programs serving Indians. The poverty programs, reservation and university technical assistance groups were dominated by whites who had pushed Indian administrators aside.

Reservation people, meanwhile, were making steady progress in spite of the numerous setbacks suffered by the national Indian community. So, in large part, younger Indian leaders who had been playing the national conference field began working at the local level to build community movements from the ground up. By consolidating local organizations into power groups, they felt that they would be in a better position to influence national thinking.

Robert Hunter, director of the Nevada Intertribal Council, had already begun to build a strong state organization of tribes and communities. In South Dakota, Gerald One Feather, Frank La-Pointe, and Ray Briggs formed the American Indian Leadership Conference, which quickly welded the educated young Sioux in that state into a strong regional organization, active in nearly every phase of Sioux life. Gerald is now running for the prestigious post of chairman of the Ogalala Sioux, the largest Sioux tribe, numbering some fifteen thousand members. Ernie Stevens, an Oneida from Wisconsin, and Lee Cook, a Chippewa from Minnesota, developed a strong program for economic and community development in Arizona. Just recently Ernie has moved into the post of director of the California Intertribal Council, a statewide organization representing some one hundred thirty thousand California Indians in cities and on the scattered reservations of that state.

By the fall of 1967 it was apparent that the national Indian scene was collapsing in favor of strong regional organizations, although the major national organizations such as the National Congress of American Indians and the National Indian Youth Council continued to grow. There was yet another factor emerging on the Indian scene: the old-timers of the depression days had educated a group of younger Indians in the old ways, and these people were now becoming a major force in Indian life. Led by Thomas Banyaca of the Hopi, Mad Bear Anderson of the Tuscarora, Clifton Hill of the Creek, and Rolling Thunder of the Shoshoni, the traditional Indians were forcing the whole Indian community to rethink its understanding of Indian life.

The message of the traditionalists is simple. They demand a return to basic Indian philosophy, establishment of ancient methods of government by open council instead of elected officials, a revival of Indian religions, and replacement of white laws with Indian customs; in short, a complete return to the ways of the old people. In an age dominated by tribalizing communications media, their message makes a great deal of sense.

But in some areas their thinking is opposed to that of the National Congress of American Indians, which represents officially elected tribal governments organized under the Indian Reorganization Act as Federal corporations. The contemporary problem is therefore one of defining the meaning of "tribe." Is it a traditionally organized band of Indians following customs with medicine men and chiefs dominating the policies of the tribe, or is it a modern corporate structure attempting to compromise at least in part with modern white culture?

The problem has been complicated by private foundations' and Government agencies' funding of Indian programs. In general this process, although it has brought a great amount of money into Indian country, has been one of cooptation.[6] Government agencies must justify their appropriation requests every year and can only take chances on spectacular programs that will serve as showcases of progress. They are not willing to invest the capital funds necessary to build viable self-supporting communities on the reservations, because these programs do not have an immediate publicity potential. Thus the Government agencies are forever committed to conducting conferences to discover that one "key" to Indian life that will give them the edge over their rival agencies in the annual appropriations derby.

Churches and foundations have merely purchased an Indian leader or program that conforms with their ideas of what Indian people should be doing. The large foundations have bought up the well-dressed, handsome "new image" Indian who is comfortable in the big cities but virtually helpless at an Indian meeting. Churches have given money to Indians who have been willing to copy black militant activist tactics, and the more violent and insulting the Indian can be, the more the churches seem to love it. They are wallowing in self-guilt and piety over the lot of the poor, yet funding demagogues of their own choosing to speak for the poor.

I did not run for re-election as excecutive director of the NCAI in the fall of 1967, but entered law school at the University of Colorado instead. It was apparent to me that the Indian revolution was well under way and that someone had better get a legal education so that we could have our own legal program for defense of Indian treaty rights. Thanks to a Ford Foundation program, nearly fifty Indians are now in law school, assuring the Indian community of legal talent in the years ahead. Within four years I foresee another radical shift in Indian leadership patterns as the growing local movements are affected by the new Indian lawyers.

There is an increasing scent of victory in the air in Indian country these days. The mood is comparable to the old days of

[6] COOPTATION: pre-empting, or seizing for oneself before others are able to do so.

the depression when the men began to dance once again. As the Indian movement gathers momentum and individual Indians cast their lot with the tribe, it will become apparent that not only will Indians survive the electronic world of Marshall McLuhan,[7] they will thrive in it. At the present time everyone is watching how mainstream America will handle the issues of pollution, poverty, crime, and racism, when it does not fundamentally understand the issues. Knowing the importance of tribal survival, Indian people are speaking more and more of sovereignty, of the great political technique of the open council, and of the need for gaining the community's consensus on all programs before putting them into effect.

One can watch this same issue emerge in white society as the "Woodstock Nation," the "Blackstone Nation,"[8] and the block organizations are developed. This is a full tribalizing process involving a nontribal people, and it is apparent that some people are frightened by it. But it is the kind of social phenomenon upon which Indians feast.

In 1965 I had a long conversation with an old Papago. I was trying to get the tribe to pay its dues to the National Congress of American Indians, and I had asked him to speak to the tribal council for me. He said that he would but that the Papago didn't really need the NCAI. They were like, he told me, the old mountain in the distance. The Spanish had come and dominated them for three hundred years and then left. The Mexicans had come and ruled them for a century, but they also left. "The Americans," he said, "have been here only about eighty years. They, too, will vanish, but the Papago and the mountain will always be here."

This attitude and understanding of life is what American society is searching for.

I wish the Government would give Alcatraz to the Indians now occupying it. They want to create five centers on the island. One center would be for a North American studies program; another would be a spiritual and medical center where Indian religions and medicines would be used and studied. A third center would

---

[7] MARSHALL McLUHAN: author of books which explore the effects upon society of worldwide electronic communication.

[8] BLACKSTONE NATION: reference to a Chicago street gang, the Blackstone Rangers, which renounced violence in 1967.

concentrate on ecological studies based on an Indian view of nature—that man should live *with* the land and not simply *on* it. A job-training center and a museum would also be founded on the island. Certain of these programs would obviously require Federal assistance.

Some people may object to this approach, yet Health, Education and Welfare gave out ten million dollars last year to non-Indians to study Indians. Not one single dollar went to an Indian scholar or researcher to present the point of view of Indian people. And the studies done by non-Indians added nothing to what was already known about Indians.

Indian people have managed to maintain a viable and cohesive social order in spite of everything the non-Indian society has thrown at them in an effort to break the tribal structure. At the same time, non-Indian society has created a monstrosity of a culture where people starve while the granaries are filled and the sun can never break through the smog.

By making Alcatraz an experimental Indian center operated and planned by Indian people, we would be given a chance to see what we could do toward developing answers to modern social problems. Ancient tribalism can be incorporated with modern technology in an urban setting. Perhaps we would not succeed in the effort, but the Government is spending billions every year and still the situation is rapidly growing worse. It just seems to a lot of Indians that this continent was a lot better off when we were running it.

FOR DISCUSSION

1. What kind of tribal system does Deloria envision as a means of improving the quality of life for Indians and non-Indians alike on the continent of North America? Do you think such a system is possible?

2. Deloria says, ". . . everyone is watching how mainstream America will handle the issues of pollution, poverty, crime, and racism, when it does not fundamentally understand the issues." What do you think he would consider a true understanding of these problems?

The Whole World Is Coming

A Ghost Dance Song

The whole world is coming.
A nation is coming, a nation is coming;
The Eagle has brought the message to the tribe.
The father says so, the father says so.
Over the whole earth they are coming.
The buffalo are coming, the buffalo are coming;
The Crow has brought the message to the tribe;
The father says so, the father says so.

LUMMI
SKAGIT
CHINOOK
KLICKITAT
SPOKAN
KALISPEL
BLACKFEET
ATSINA
ASSINIBOIN
HIDATSA
MANDAN
ARIKARA
THE
NORTHERN
FISHERMEN
YAKIMA
UMATILLA
NEZ PERCE
KUTENAI
FLATHEAD
CROW
CHEYENNE
SIOUX
SIOUX
KAROK
KLAMATH
SHOSHONI
BANNOCK
ARAPAHO
SIOUX
OMAHA
PONCA
HUPA
WINTUN
PAIUTE
SHOSHONI
POMO
WASHO
SHOSHONI
UTE
GOSIUTE
THE SEED GATHERERS
THE HUNTERS OF THE PLAINS
OSAGE
TOLOWA
PAIUTE
PAIUTE
UTE
PONCA
HOPI
HAVASUPAI
WALAPAI
THE NAVAHO
SHEPHERDS
THE
PUEBLO
FARMERS
CADDO
WICHITA
OTO
PAWNEE
IOWA
MISSION
MARICOPA
PIMA
PAPAGO
APACHE
CHEYENNE
ARAPAHO
KIOWA
COMANCHE
MOHAVE
YUMA
CHEMEHUEVI
THE DESERT DWELLERS
APACHE

SOME MAJOR TRIBES

CHIPPEWA
CHIPPEWA
CHIPPEWA
CHIPPEWA
CHIPPEWA
MENOMINEE
CHIPPEWA
STOCKBRIDGES
OTTAWA
POTAWATOMI
POTAWATOMI
WINNEBAGO
FOXES
WINNEBAGO
CHIPPEWA
MIAMI
POTAWATOMI
KICKAPOO
SAUK
IOWA
OTTAWA
SENECA
SHAWNEE
QUAPAW
WYANDOT

PENOBSCOT
PASSAMAQUODDY
IROQUOIS
NARRAGANSET
IROQUOIS
WAMPANOAG
MOHEGAN
PEQUOT
IROQUOIS
MONTAUK
NANTICOKE
POWHATAN
SUSQUEHANNA
NOTTAWAY

THE WOODSMEN OF THE EASTERN FORESTS

MACHAPUNGA
CHEROKEE
CATAWBA

CHEROKEE
CREEK
SEMINOLE
CHOCTAW
CHICKASAW
KICKAPOO
SAUK
POTAWATOMI
CHOCTAW
ALABAMA
KOASATI
HOUMA
TUNICA
CREEK
CHITIMACHA

SEMINOLE

AND THEIR LOCATIONS

147

Major Tribes in the United States

Alabama. Abihka, Alabama, Apalachee, Apalachicola, Atasi, Chatot, Cherokee, Chickasaw, Choctaw, Eufaula, Fus-hatchee, Hilibi, Hitchiti, Kan-hatki, Kealidji, Koasati, Kolomi, Mobile, Muklasa, Muskogee, Napochi, Natchez, Okchai, Okmulgee, Osochi, Pakana, Pawokti, Pilthlako, Sawokli, Shawnee, Taensa, Tohome, Tukabahchee, Tuskegee, Wakokai, Wiwohka, Yamasee, Yuchi

Alaska. Ahtena, Dihai-kutchin, Eskimo, Haida, Han, Ingalik, Koyukon, Kutchakutchin, Nabesna, Niska, Natsit-kutchin, Tanaina, Tanana, Tennuth-kutchin, Tlingit, Tranjik-kutchin, Tsimshian, Vunta-kutchin

Arizona. Apache, Cocopa, Halchidhoma, Halyikwamai, Havasupai, Hopi, Kohuana, Maricopa, Mohave, Navaho or Navajo, Paiute, Papago, Pima, Quahatika, Sobaipuri, Tonto, Walapai, Yavapai, Yuma

Arkansas. Caddo, Cahinnio, Cherokee, Chickasaw, Choctaw, Illinois, Kaskinampo, Michigamea, Ofo or Mosopelea, Osage, Quapaw, Tunica, Yazoo

California. Achomawi, Alliklik, Atsugewi, Bear River Indians, Cahuilla, Chemehuevi, Chetco, Chilula, Chimariko, Chumash, Costanoan, Cupeño, Dakubetede, Diegueño, Esselen, Fernandeño, Gabrielino, Halchidhoma, Huchnom, Hupa, Juaneño, Kamia, Karok, Kato, Kawaiisu, Kitanemuk, Konomihu, Koso, Lassik, Luiseño, Maidu, Mattole, Mission Creek, Miwok, Modoc, Mohave, Nicoleño, Nongati, Okwanuchu, Paiute, Patwin, Pomo, Serrano, Shasta, Sinkyone, Tolowa, Tübatulabal, Vanyume, Wailaki, Wappo, Washo, Whilkut, Wintu, Wintun, Wiyot, Yahi, Yana, Yokuts, Yuki, Yuki (Coast)

Colorado. Apache, Arapaho, Bannock, Cheyenne, Comanche, Jicarilla, Kiowa, Kiowa Apache, Navaho, Pueblo, Shoshoni, Ute

Connecticut. Mahican, Mohegan, Niantic, Nipmuc, Pequot, Wappinger

Delaware. Delaware, Nanticoke

Florida. Acuera, Aguacaleyquen, Ais, Alabama, Amacano, Amacapiras or Macapiras, Apalachee, Apalachicola, Calusa, Caparaz, Chatot, Chiaha, Chilucan, Chine, Creek, Fresh Water Indians, Guacata, Guale, Hitchiti, Icafui, Jeaga, Koasati, Mikasaki, Mococo or Mucoço, Muklasa, Muskogee, Ocale or Etocale, Oconee, Onatheaqua, Osochi, Pawokti, Pensacola, Pohoy or Pooy, Potano, Saturiwa, Sawoklee, Seminole, Surruque, Tecatacuru, Tawasa, Tekesta or Tequesta, Tocobaga, Ucita, Utina or Timucua, Yamasee, Yuchi, Yufera, Yui, Yustaga

Georgia. Apalachee, Apalachicola, Chatot, Cherokee, Chiaha, Chickasaw, Creek, Guale, Hitchiti, Kasihta, Oconee, Okmulgee, Osochi, Sawokli, Shawnee, Tamathli, Timucua, Yamasee, Yuchi, Yufera

Idaho. Bannock, Kalispel, Kutenai, Nez Percé, Paiute, Palouse, Salish or Flathead, Shoshoni, Skitswish, Snakes, Spokan

Illinois. Chippewa or Ojibway, Delaware, Foxes, Illinois, Kickapoo, Miami, Ottawa, Potawatomi, Sauk, Shawnee, Winnebago, Wyandot or Huron

Indiana. Chippewa, Delaware, Erie, Illinois, Iroquois, Kickapoo, Miami, Mosopelea, Neutrals, Ottawa, Potawatomi, Shawnee, Wyandot

Iowa. Chippewa, Dakota or Sioux, Foxes, Illinois, Iowa, Missouri, Moingwena, Omaha, Oto, Ottawa, Peoria, Ponca, Potawatomi, Sauk, Winnebago

Kansas. Apache, Arapaho, Cherokee, Cheyenne, Chippewa, Comanche, Delaware, Foxes, Illinois, Iowa, Iroquois, Kansa, Kickapoo, Kiowa, Kiowa Apache, Miami, Missouri, Munsee, Osage, Oto, Ottawa, Pawnee, Potawatomi, Quapaw, Sauk, Shawnee, Wyandot

Kentucky. Cherokee, Chickasaw, Mosopelea, Shawnee, Yuchi

Louisiana. Acolapissa, Adai, Alabama, Apalachee, Atakapa, Avoyel, Bayogoula, Biloxi, Caddo, Chatot, Chawasha, Chitimacha, Choctaw, Doustioni, Houma, Koasati, Koroa, Mugulasha, Muskogee, Natchez, Ofo, Okelousa, Opelousa, Ouachita, Pascagoula, Quapaw, Quinipissa, Souchitioni, Taensa, Tangipahoa, Tawasa, Washa, Yatasi

Maine. Abnaki, Malecite, Passamaquoddy, Pennacook, Penobscot

Maryland and District of Columbia. Conoy, Delaware, Nanticoke, Powhatan, Shawnee, Susquehanna

Massachusetts. Mahican, Massachuset, Nauset, Nipmuc, Pennacook, Pocomtuc, Wampanoag

Michigan. Chippewa, Foxes, Kickapoo, Menominee, Miami, Neutrals, Noquet, Ottawa, Potawatomi, Sauk, Wyandot

Minnesota. Arapaho, Cheyenne, Chippewa, Dakota, Foxes, Iowa, Missouri, Omaha, Oto, Ottawa, Ponca, Sauk, Winnebago, Wyandot

Mississippi. Acolapissa, Biloxi, Capinans, Chakchiuma, Chickasaw, Choctaw, Choula, Grigra, Houma, Ibitoupa, Koasati, Koroa, Moctobi, Natchez, Ofo or Ofogoula, Okelousa, Pascagoula, Pensacola, Quapaw, Taposa, Tiou, Tunica, Yazoo

Missouri. Caddo, Dakota, Delaware, Foxes, Illinois, Iowa, Kickapoo, Missouri, Omaha, Osage, Oto, Sauk, Shawnee

Montana. Arapaho, Arikara or Ree, Assiniboin Sioux, Atsina or Gros Ventre, Bannock, Cheyenne, Chippewa, Cree, Crow, Dakota, Hidatsa, Kalispel, Kiowa, Kutenai, Mandan, Nez Percé, Salish, Sematuse, Shoshoni, Siksika or Blackfeet, Spokan, Tunahe

Nebraska. Arapaho, Arikara, Cheyenne, Comanche, Dakota, Foxes, Iowa, Kansa, Kiowa, Missouri, Omaha, Oto, Pawnee, Ponca, Sauk, Winnebago

Nevada. Koso, Paiute, Pueblo, Shoshoni, Ute, Washo

New Hampshire. Abnaki, Pennacook

New Jersey. Delaware

New Mexico. Apache, Comanche, Jemez, Keresan Pueblo, Kiowa, Kiowa Apache, Lipan, Manso, Navaho, Peco, Piro Pueblo, Shuman, Tewa Pueblo, Tiwa Pueblo, Ute, Zuñi

New York. Cayuga Iroquois, Delaware, Erie, Mahican, Mohawk Iroquois, Mohegan, Montauk, Neutrals, Oneida Iroquois, Onondaga Iroquois, Saponi, Seneca Iroquois, Tuscarora, Tutelo, Wappinger, Wenrohronon

North Carolina. Bear River Indians, Cape Fear Indians, Catawba, Cheraw or Sara, Cherokee, Chowanoc, Coree or Coranine, Eno, Hatteras, Keyauwee, Machapunga, Meherrin, Moratok, Natchez, Neusiok, Occaneechi, Pamlico, Saponi, Shakori, Sissipahaw, Sugeree, Tuscarora, Tutelo, Waccamaw, Wateree, Waxhaw, Weapemeoc or Yeopim, Woccon, Yadkin

North Dakota. Arapaho, Arikara, Assiniboin Sioux, Cheyenne, Chippewa, Dakota, Hidatsa, Mandan

Ohio. Chippewa, Delaware, Erie, Honniasont, Illinois, Iroquois, Kickapoo, Miami, Mosopelea, Neutrals, Ottawa, Potawatomi, Shawnee, Wyandot

Oklahoma. Alabama, Apache, Apalachee, Arapaho, Biloxi, Caddo, Cherokee, Cheyenne, Chickasaw, Choctaw, Comanche, Creek, Delaware, Foxes, Hitchiti, Illinois, Iowa, Iroquois, Jicarilla, Kansa, Kichai, Kickapoo, Kiowa, Kiowa Apache, Koasati, Lipan, Miami, Mikusaki, Missouri, Modoc, Muklasa, Munsee, Muskogee, Natchez, Nez Percé, Okmulgee, Osage, Oto, Ottawa, Pawnee, Peoria, Ponca, Potawatomi, Quapaw, Sauk, Seminole, Shawnee, Tawakoni, Tawehash, Tonkawa, Tuskegee, Waco, Wichita, Wyandot, Yscani, Yuchi

Oregon. Ahantchuyuk, Alsea, Atfalati, Bannock, Calapooya, Chastacosta, Chelamela, Chepenafa, Chetco, Clackamas, Clatskanie, Clatsop, Clowwewalla, Dakubetede, Hanis, Klamath, Kuitsh, Latgawa, Lohim, Luckiamute or Lakmiut, Miluk, Mishikhwutmetunne, Modoc, Molala, Multnomah, Naltunnetunne, Nez Percé, Paiute, Santiam, Shasta, Siletz, Siuslaw, Skilloot, Snake, Takelma, Taltushtuntude, Tenino, Tillamook, Tututni, Tyigh, Umatilla, Umpqua, Wallawalla, Walpapi, Wasco, Watlala, Yahuskin, Yamel, Yaquina, Yoncalla

Pennsylvania. Delaware, Erie, Honniasont, Iroquois, Saluda, Saponi, Shawnee, Susquehanna, Tuscarora, Tutelo, Wenrohronon

Rhode Island. Narraganset, Niantic, Nipmuc, Pequot, Wampanoag

South Carolina. Catawba, Cherokee, Chiaha, Chickasaw, Congaree, Creek, Cusabo, Eno, Keyauwee, Natchez, Pedee, Saluda, Santee Sioux, Sewee, Shakori, Shawnee, Sissipahaw, Sugeree, Waccamaw, Wateree, Waxhaw, Winyaw, Yamasee, Yuchi

South Dakota. Arapaho, Arikara, Cheyenne, Dakota, Kiowa, Mandan, Omaha, Ponca, Sutaio, Winnebago

Tennessee. Catawba, Cherokee, Chiaha, Chickasaw, Kaskinampo, Mosopelea, Muskogee, Natchez, Shawnee, Tali, Tuskegee, Yuchi

Texas. Akokisa, Alabama, Anadarko, Apache, Aranama, Bidai, Biloxi, Caddo, Cherokee, Choctaw, Coahuiltecan Tribes, Comanche, Creek, Deadose, Eyeish or Háish, Guasco, Hainai, Hasinai Confederacy, Kadohadacho Confederacy, Karankawan Tribes, Kichai or Kitsei, Kiowa, Koasati, Lipan, Muskogee, Nanatsoho, Nasoni, Pakana, Pascagoula, Patiri, Pueblo, Quapaw, Shawnee, Shuman, Soacatino or Xacatin, Tawakoni, Tonkawan Tribes, Waco, Wichita

Utah. Bannock, Gosiute, Navaho, Paiute, Shoshoni, Ute

Vermont. Abnaki, Mahican, Pennacook, Pocomtuc

Virginia. Cherokee, Manahoac, Meherrin, Monacan, Nahyssan, Nottaway, Occaneechi, Powhatan, Saponi, Shakori, Shawnee, Tutelo

Washington. Cathlamet, Cathlapotle, Cayuse, Chehalis, Chellan, Chilluckittequaw, Chemakum, Chinook, Clackamas, Clallam, Clalskanie, Columbia or Sinkiuse-Columbia, Colville, Copalis, Cowlitz, Duwamish, Hoh, Humptulips, Kalispel, Klickitat, Kwaiailk, Kwalhioqua, Lummi, Makah, Methow, Mical, Muckleshoot, Neketemeuk, Nespelem, Nez Percé, Nisqually, Nooksack, Ntlakyapamuk, Okanagon, Ozette, Palouse, Pshwanwapam, Puyallup, Queets or Quaitso, Quilcute, Sahehwamish, Samish, Sanpoil, Satsop, Semiahmoo, Senijextee, Sinkaietk, Sinkakaius, Skagit, Skilloot, Skin, Snohomish, Snoqualmie, Spokan, Squaxon or Squakson, Suquamish, Swallah, Swinomish, Taidnapam, Twana, Wallawalla, Wanapam, Watlala, Wauyukma, Wenatchee, Wishram, Wynoochee, Yakima

West Virginia. Moneton, Cherokee, Conoy, Delaware, Honniasont, Susquehanna, Shawnee

Wisconsin. Chippewa, Dakota, Foxes, Housatonic, Illinois, Iowa, Iroquois, Kickapoo, Mahican, Mascouten, Menominee, Miami, Missouri, Munsee, Noquet, Oto, Ottawa, Potawatomi, Sauk, Stockbridges, Tionontati, Winnebago, Wyandot

Wyoming. Arapaho, Bannock, Cheyenne, Comanche, Crow, Dakota, Kiowa, Kiowa Apache, Pawnee, Shoshoni, Ute